Faithful to the End!

Living as Jesus' Disciples in the Last Days

Reuven & Yanit Ross

Faithful till the End

Most scriptural quotations are taken from the Holy Bible, New King James Version. Copyright © 1982 by Thomas Nelson, Inc.

Proofread by Alison Neubert, Waco, TX

Layout and design of book cover by Kudzai Musumhi, Carbondale, IL.

Layout and design of book text by Reuven Ross
ISBN-13: 978-1986160919, copyright © 2018

Printed in the USA by CreateSpace, an Amazon.com Company

Website: www.making-disciples.net
Email: reuven@making-disciples.net
           yanit@making-disciples.net

TABLE OF CONTENTS

Introduction

Song – Days of Elijah

INTRODUCTION

For many years, we have taught on discipleship and the call to be holy unto the Lord. In 2016, the Holy Spirit led us to begin teaching about the second coming of Jesus and what the days preceding His return will be like. We taught for many months on the importance of living faithfully as Jesus' disciples in the difficult, stressful times that herald His coming. The result of all that teaching is this book.

The first disciples asked Jesus: *"What will be the sign of Your coming* (to set up Your throne on earth as Messiah and King) *and of the end of the age* (of Roman occupation and oppression)*?"* (**Matt. 24:3**). They wanted to know when Jesus would return as Sovereign to restore their liberties and fortunes and to rule in Israel. Jesus answered those questions in Matthew 24-25, the chapters on which most of this book is based.

In the Scriptures, we are given clear warnings of what we can expect of the Last Days. It is easy to see that we are now in the birth pangs of the Day of the Lord; the signs He warned us of are increasing. We believe this is the time to strategically prepare *"to endure to the end"* (Matt. 24:13). Because the Lord is coming for a spotless Bride who loves Him with all of her heart, we must deal now with heart issues and lifestyle choices that do not line up with His Word and will. We need to fix our gaze on the life to come, rather than keeping our feet and focus firmly planted on this earth. Jesus is returning for a faithful bride who is stunningly beautiful in devotion and purity. We need to make ourselves ready!

Faithful disciples of Jesus Christ

How do we stay faithful in a world of unfaithfulness?

How do we stay pure in a carnal, sex-crazed society?

How do we lay down our lives sacrificially for the salvation of others when our self-centered cultures encourage us to indulge ourselves and pursue comfort and convenience?

While death is promoted by euthanasia, abortion, and suicide, how do we boldly stand for life?

In cities and nations where many people have a sense of entitlement, how do we responsibly work hard to provide for our families and have enough to give generously to the poor and to missions?

Even though idolatry abounds, we are *still* to love the Lord our God with all our hearts, souls, minds, and strength! God's call on His people to be righteous and uncompromisingly holy is just as strong today as it has ever been. *"As He who called you is holy, you also be holy in all your conduct, because it is written, 'Be holy, for I am holy' "* (**1 Pet. 1:15-16**).

The Holy Spirit warns us that in the last days perilous times will come. Those days will be tough, strenuous, and dangerous. He gave a clear description of this time in **2 Tim. 3:1-5, 13**.

> *"For men will be lovers of themselves* (selfish), *lovers of money* (greedy, covetous), *boasters, proud* (arrogant), *blasphemers* (hateful against God and man), *disobedient to parents, unthankful, unholy, unloving* (without natural affection for family and relatives), *unforgiving* (irreconcilable), *slanderers, without self-control, brutal* (fierce, savage), *despisers of good* (hostile to virtue), *traitors* (betrayers), *headstrong, haughty* (conceited), *lovers of pleasure rather than* (more than) *lovers of God, having a form of godliness but denying its power* (appearing righteous, but rejecting and refusing the miraculous power of God). *And from such people turn away* (avoid them)... *Evil men and impostors will grow worse and worse, deceiving and being deceived."*

Times of the Gentiles

In **Luke 21:24** Jesus said, *"And they will fall by the edge of the sword, and be led away captive into all nations. And Jerusalem will be trampled by Gentiles* (non-Jews) *until the times of the Gentiles are fulfilled."* The "times of the Gentiles" were fulfilled when Jerusalem was no longer in the control of non-Jewish nations.

A new era began on God's calendar when the Jews recaptured Jerusalem in 1967. If we want to see where we are in salvation's history, we must keep our eyes on Israel. Many, if not most, spiritual leaders in the Church today believe we have transitioned into what is called "the Last Days."

The believers living when Jesus returns will see the greatest revival and the most severe pressures. The coming months and years will be extremely difficult, but they will also be glorious! In the midst of the greatest opposition will be the greatest breakthroughs and victories.

Isaiah 60:2 says, *"For behold, the darkness shall cover the earth, and deep darkness the people; but the Lord will arise over you, and His glory will be seen upon you."* Deep darkness and glory will come together in the Last Days. There will be an unleashing of demonic activity in the earth. Depravity, perversion, and sin will reach unbelievably wicked levels. There will also be an outpouring of the Holy Spirit as prophesied in Joel 2:28-32. Millions and millions of people will be swept into the kingdom of God as the final great harvest is reaped.

What awesome days we are living in! This is not the time to shrink back from seeking and doing God's will. It's not the time to coddle and pamper our flesh. This is when we need to seek God fervently! We must rid ourselves of all sin and compromise and throw off the weights of shame and complacency. This is when we need to engage in good works, share the gospel freely and widely, and aggressively push God's kingdom forward through prayer and worship.

The King is coming! Let's prepare for Him and make His way ready! Let's lift up our heads with courage and joy. Soon we shall be *forever* with the Lord!

Reuven & Yanit

"And I heard, as it were, the voice of a great multitude, as the sound of many waters and as the sound of mighty thundering, saying, 'Alleluia! For the Lord God Omnipotent reigns! Let us be glad and rejoice and give Him glory, for the marriage of the Lamb has come, and His wife has made herself ready.' And it was granted for her to be arrayed in fine linen, clean and bright, for the fine linen is the righteous acts of the saints. Then he said to me, 'Write: Blessed are those who are called to the marriage supper of the Lamb!' " (**Rev. 19:6-9a**).

DAYS OF ELIJAH

Robin Mark wrote *Days of Elijah* in 1994. Someone wrote the third verse sometime later. This was our class theme song for 2016 while we taught on the subjects in this book.

These are the days of Elijah,
Declaring the word of the Lord.
And these are the days of Your servant Moses,
Righteousness being restored.
And though these are days of great trial,
Of famine and darkness and sword,
Still, we are the voice in the desert crying,
'Prepare ye the way of the Lord!'

Chorus: *Behold He comes riding on the clouds,*
Shining like the sun at the trumpet call!
Lift your voice it's the year of Jubilee,
And out of Zion's hill salvation comes!

These are the days of Ezekiel,
The dry bones becoming as flesh;
And these are the days of Your servant David,
Rebuilding a temple of praise.
And these are the days of the harvest,
The fields are white in Your world,
And we are the laborers in Your vineyard,
Declaring the word of the Lord!

These are the days of Isaiah,
"Here am I, Lord, send me."
And these are the days of Your servant, Peter,
Preaching the gospel of Christ.
And these are the days of outpouring,
Your sons and your daughters sent forth
And we will go forth into the conflict trusting,
Declaring the Word of the Lord!

There's no God like Yeshua! (6x)

If these are the days of Elijah, then we need to be the Elijahs of our day, declaring the word of the Lord! *We* are the voice in the desert, crying, "Prepare the way of the Lord!"

This song speaks of many themes that are central today: declaration of truth, integrity, righteousness, justice, unity in the Body of Christ, and worship. "Days of great trial, of famine, darkness and sword" is a reflection of this season when thousands of people die every day from starvation, malnutrition, terrorism, and war. In the midst of it all, we are to declare the truth of what we believe. We need to make a stand for justice and righteousness.

The "days of the Harvest" speak of the call we share as believers—to make disciples of Jesus in every nation. "The fields are white in the world" means they are ripe for harvest. It is urgent that we make known the gospel of the kingdom of God to the millions who are lost and in need of salvation.

The chorus is the ultimate declaration of our hope—our Messiah's return. Let's make sure we are prepared to meet Him! As His Bride, let's make ourselves ready!

Chapter 1

A PEOPLE PREPARED FOR THE LORD

John the Baptist was born at a very strategic time in human history. It was said of John, *"And he will turn many of the children of Israel to the Lord their God. He will also go before Him in the spirit and power of Elijah 'to turn the hearts of the fathers to the children,' and the disobedient to the wisdom of the just, to make ready a people prepared for the Lord"* (**Luke 1:16-17**).

John was preparing people for the Lord by preaching repentance and proclaiming the coming of the Lamb of God Who would take away the sin of the world. John was baptizing people from Jerusalem, Judea, and all around the Jordan River as they confessed their sin and repented.

Spiritual leaders in Jerusalem sent priests and Levites to ask John who he was (John 1:19). They asked if he were the Messiah or Elijah or "the Prophet." They wanted to put a title on him and give him a name. In response to their question of *"What do you say about yourself?"* John simply said, *"I am a voice"* (John 1:23). His desire was to prepare the way for the name of Jesus Christ, not to make a name for himself.

John didn't want a great reputation or title, nor did he yield to the pride that can easily come with a successful ministry. In spite of multiple thousands of people hearing his preaching and responding to his message and ministry, he refused the praises of men. This voice from the wilderness continued perfectly on course to prepare the Lord's people for the coming of their Messiah.

John was *"the voice of one crying in the wilderness; prepare the way of the Lord; make straight in the desert a highway for our God"* (**Isa. 40:3**). He was not the Light (Messiah), but was sent to bear witness of the Light (John 1:6-8). He expected those who responded to his plea for repentance to turn from sin and rebellion to obedience to God's commandments.

1

we were born in a very strategic time in human history! As
Jesus, we have a prophetic call on our lives to prepare people
nd coming of the Messiah, Jesus. So, we need to preach
d proclaim the Lord's return. We know we're nothing in and
ourselves, so we don't take pride in our call or ministry activity. We
know we are sent to bear witness of the Light.

We face the same choice John faced—to make a name for ourselves or to
be a voice for the Lord. *This is the time to be a voice,* preparing the way of
the Lord. It is not the time to build reputations or to assume great names or
titles. The one name we want to exalt is Jesus Christ, the Lamb of God,
the Savior of the world, and the glory of Israel! Jesus came first to bring
salvation to all who would believe; He will come the second time as Judge
and Lord of all. Knowing this, we can't help but plead with everyone: *be
reconciled to God!*

Jerusalem, Israel

Because of the signs around us, including the rebirth of Israel as a nation
in 1948 and the reunification of Jerusalem as it's capital in 1967, we see
that we are drawing close to our Lord's return. To know where we are on
God's prophetic timetable, it is important that we know and understand
what is happening in Israel. Israel is God's timepiece.

The writers of the New Testament were an apocalyptic people. They
expected Jesus to return soon and lived with purpose and intentionality.
That was almost 2000 years ago; how much closer is His return today! We
see the signs of the times; let's not ignore them foolishly. We must live
wisely in this significant hour of history.

Prophecy of the Temple's Destruction

*"Then Jesus went out and departed from the temple, and His disciples came
up to show Him the buildings of the temple. And Jesus said to them, 'Do you
not see all these things? Assuredly, I say to you, not one stone shall be left
here upon another, that shall not be thrown down.'"* (**Matt. 24:1-2**).

This prophecy of Jesus was fulfilled less than 40 years later when the temple was destroyed. In 70 AD, on the ninth of Av on the Hebrew calendar, Roman soldiers set fire to the temple in Jerusalem, changing the course of Judaism up until this present time. The previous temple located in the same place was destroyed on the same day centuries earlier. Jews around the world still commemorate the ninth of Av as the saddest day of the year.

Since 70 AD, there has been no temple, no sacrifices, and no priestly function within the temple. However, in recent years, the articles and furniture for the third temple have been built and prepared. The men of the tribe of Levi are being trained as priests in Jerusalem. Priestly garments have been made. Perfect lambs for sacrifice are being intentionally raised. The Jews are hoping that soon they can rebuild a third temple and worship on the Temple Mount once again. These are major signs of the Last Days!

Set apart for God

As a voice to the Church, we need to live with priorities that befit the kingdom of God. We are to eagerly and sacrificially do good works. Our lives should model humility and fervent prayer. We must be faithful in the midst of increasing persecution, and serve the Lord effectively during the international revival that will accompany that persecution. *And* we must be ready to meet the Lord in death when He calls us—with no unfinished business, reconciled with loved ones, and having our lives in order.

This world is not our home; we are just passing through as sojourners. We must not get entangled with worldly affairs; we need to stay focused on the goal for the prize of the high calling of God in Jesus Christ (Phil. 3:14). While we are here, it is our privilege and responsibility to share God's love and salvation. Once we change our residence to Heaven, we can no longer share the gospel with anyone—everyone there will be saved! We cannot die to self so that others can live; we can't suffer for His great name; we cannot forgive those who offend us; we can't serve by cleaning or cooking for others. We can't pay our tithes or give offerings to missions. All of that is part of our life on earth; it has no place in Heaven. We need to do those things here while we can! *"For in death there is no remembrance of You; in the grave who will give You thanks?"* (**Ps. 6:5**).

An eternal mindset

Knowing Jesus personally should dictate our perspective on life. We are set apart by God for God. If we do not see this clearly, we might live for this present time rather than for eternity with the Lord. We may strive to be successful in this life rather than try to win souls for the life to come. To expend ourselves for this life *only* is to be shortsighted. This is merely the dressing room where we prepare for the main event—eternal life in Heaven. *"Set your mind on things above, not on things on the earth. For you died, and your life is hidden with Christ in God"* (**Col. 3:2-3**).

Living for eternity is having God's love for people, and being willing to pay any price to escort them into a relationship with Him. It motivates us to live simply so that we can invest more generously into the Lord's work. Knowing this world is passing away, we should wisely prepare for the life to come. We are to use our time, talents, and finances to build the Lord's kingdom, not our own.

Aware of our immortality

"All flesh is grass, and all its loveliness is like the flower of the field. The grass withers, the flower fades, because the breath of the Lord blows upon it; surely the people are grass. The grass withers, the flower fades, but the word of our God stands forever" (**Isa. 40:6b-8**).

With Jesus' return being imminent and things on earth moving rapidly toward closure, we need to urgently proclaim to others that life here is temporary and passing away. Only what is done for and with Jesus Christ will count eternally. As we can, we need to equip God's people to maneuver through the coming difficult days as true disciples. Knowing the seriousness of this time should provoke us to think deeply, pray passionately, plan carefully, and live intentionally.

The glory of God on His people and the darkness in the earth will grow together in the Last Days. This is to be the Church's finest hour as she shines triumphantly. The Last Days are and will be the most exciting and the most demanding for those who carry the Lord's name. May we prove ourselves to be faithful!

4

Chapter 2

SIGNS OF HIS COMING

Jesus' disciples asked Him: *"What will be the sign of Your coming and of the end of the age?"* (**Matt. 24:3b**). In reply, Jesus began to tell them of the signs that signal His approaching return. His response as recorded in **Luke 21:25** was: *"And there will be signs in the sun, in the moon, and in the stars; and on the earth distress of nations, with perplexity, the sea and the waves roaring."*

The Amplified Bible reads: *"And there will be signs in the sun and moon and stars; and upon the earth [there will be] distress (trouble and anguish) of nations in bewilderment and perplexity [without resources, left wanting, in doubt, not knowing which way to turn] at the roaring of the tossing of the sea, men swooning away or expiring with fear and dread and apprehension and expectation of the things that are coming on the world; for the [very] powers of the heavens will be shaken and caused to totter. And then they will see the Son of Man coming in a cloud with great (transcendent and overwhelming) power and [kingly] glory (majesty and splendor)"* (**Luke 21:25-27**).

A prominent Rabbi in Israel, Yosef Berger, said in November 2017: "The world is entering a new period leading up to the Messiah, and the old rules no longer apply. The laws of nature have been cancelled out, and we are seeing a time when natural disasters are commonplace. Rules of how people act, even in the worst of circumstances, have changed."

Signs in the earth and sky

One of the worst signs in the earth (and sea) in recent years was the tsunami that hit the coasts of the Indian Ocean on December 26, 2004. It was the deadliest and most published natural disaster in modern history. At least 290,000 people, including tourists from all over the world, were killed or missing in 14 countries bordering the Indian Ocean.

Jesus also said there will be "signs in the moon." Historic signs were seen globally in 2014 and 2015 when four Blood Moons appeared.

All four took place on the first day of two major biblical feasts of the Lord: on the first night of Passover in April and on the first night of the Feast of Tabernacles in October. Each time, the moon turned orange-red.

Israeli astronomer, Ira Machefsky, has 60 years of experience leading stargazing tours in Mizpeh Ramon, a town next to a huge crater in the Negev desert of Israel. Machefsky sees the divine importance of heavenly events. "The Talmud states that a *Likui* (eclipse) of the sun is a bad sign for the world, but a lunar eclipse is a bad sign for Israel," Machefsky said to journalists of *Breaking Israel News* in May 2017.

In August 2017, there was a solar eclipse in the USA, the first one in 99 years. Many rabbis and evangelical pastors were attributing various meanings to the eclipse. One thing we know for certain: it is a sign in the heavens that our Creator does exist! Our lives on earth are no accident. We have a sovereign God in Heaven who is to be feared and worshiped!

Distress of nations

Jesus spoke of "distress of nations, with perplexity." The increase of terrorism and violence is causing distress in numerous nations. The threats by North Korea and Iran, the terrorism in the Middle East, and the civil conflict in nations are further signs that Jesus' return is approaching. Perilous times are upon us, and, as Jesus warned, they will increase.

Dr. Dave Williams says, "The generation that sees these signs taking place simultaneously and globally will be part of the final generation, and they will possibly experience the long awaited return of Jesus Christ. While followers of Christ will walk in hope, faith, and great power, others will taste only anguish and distress in the days ahead."

Increase of hurricanes

The hyperactive 2017 Atlantic hurricane season featured the highest total accumulated cyclone energy (ACE) and the highest number of major hurricanes since 2005. It had the greatest number of consecutive hurricanes in the satellite era, all reaching winds of at least 75 mph (120 km/h). It was the most destructive season on record, with a preliminary total of over $316.51 billion (USD) in damages, nearly all of which was due to three of the major hurricanes of the season—Harvey, Irma, and Maria.

This season was also one of only six years on record to feature multiple Category 5 hurricanes. Irma's landfalls on multiple Caribbean islands and Maria's landfall on Dominica make 2017 the second season on record (after 2007) to feature two hurricanes making landfall at Category 5 intensity. In addition, Irma was the strongest hurricane ever recorded to form in the Atlantic Ocean outside of the Gulf of Mexico and the Caribbean Sea. This season is the only one on record in which three hurricanes each had an ACE of over 40: Irma, Jose, and Maria.

Decline of morality

There is a sharp decline of morality in the USA and in other western nations. Perversions are almost accepted as normal, and gay marriage has been legalized in many places. Even some Christian universities and seminaries have stepped back from speaking out against immorality.

As of 2017, over 60 million babies have been aborted in the United States since the court case of Roe vs. Wade in 1973. This is a terrible slaughter of innocent human life! Moral values in the USA have been eroding for years. Pornography is rampant and millions of Americans are addicted to it, including multitudes of Christians and spiritual leaders. America, once a God-fearing nation, is in a moral crisis.

Another sign of the times is the many entertainments, amusements, and diversions that keep believers from attending prayer meetings and zealously seeking after God. Many believers have become indifferent, uninterested, and unconcerned about the corruption around us. As followers and disciples of the Lord Jesus, we have a responsibility not to let our hearts become distracted by the world. We must keep our desires aligned with eternity.

Spiritual awakening in the nations

For years, modern prophets have spoken of a major move of God in the earth preceding Jesus' return. That is happening now! There are pockets of revival and the beginnings of spiritual awakenings in numerous countries.

In China, approximately 1200 nationals are saved and baptized in water every day. Believers there now number over 130 million! For years, discipleship materials and Bibles were scarce in China, but now they are more readily available.

A headline in the UK *Telegraph* April 14, 2014 read: "China on course to become 'world's most Christian nation' within 15 years. The number of Christians in Communist China is growing so steadily that it by 2030 it could have more churchgoers than America."

Amazing revivals are taking place in Iraq and Syria. Multitudes of people from the Assyrian Church of Iraqis and Kurds, who had not had a personal relationship with Christ, are now finding salvation in Jesus. Many Muslims are embracing Jesus as Lord after seeing brave Christians face martyrdom with joy and peace. Others are coming to faith in Jesus as Messiah because of the visions and dreams God is giving them.

God is drawing Iranians to Himself. The underground church movement in Iran is growing despite the regime's crackdown on Christians. Hundreds are being baptized in large ceremonies. Elam Ministries says twenty years ago, Iran had only 2000–5000 believers, but statistics in 2016 reveal that there could be up to one million believers there now.

Another source, Fox News, said in 2016: "The number of Muslim converts who are risking prison or death by secretly worshipping as Christians in Iran's house church movement has grown to as many as one million people, according to watchdog groups." The house church movement is seeing astounding growth despite the intense persecution it faces from the government. According to a few sources, there are at least 22,000 house churches in Iran.

The website of R. Safa (a former Iranian, Shiite Muslim, but now an evangelical pastor) says, "Despite severe persecution by the Iranian government against underground churches, God's Word is spreading like a wildfire all over Iran. Iranian Muslims are converting to Christianity at an unprecedented pace, perhaps by the thousands every day. Pastor Safa believes that Iran will be the first Islamic nation to convert to Christianity."

On the African continent, at least six million people come to faith in Jesus every year. A 2012 Pew Research report claimed that, "The share of the population that is Christian in sub-Saharan Africa climbed from 9 percent in 1910 to 63 percent in 2010." Much of this growth occurred in the midst of Muslim-majority populations.

In Israel, the Body of Messiah is growing steadily and rapidly with at least 25,000-30,000 believers attending Messianic congregations, and 4000-5000 Arab Evangelical Christians openly worshiping the Lord. God is calling out a people for Himself!

Joel 2:28-29, 32a says, *"And it shall come to pass afterward that I will pour out My Spirit on all flesh; your sons and your daughters shall prophesy, your old men shall dream dreams, your young men shall see visions. And also on My menservants and on My maidservants I will pour out My Spirit in those days... And it shall come to pass that whoever calls on the name of the Lord shall be saved."*

Prayer movements

Another current move of God is in the establishing of 24/7 Prayer Houses. There are hundreds of underground Prayer Houses in nations where persecution of believers exists. These we cannot document in order to ensure their safety, but there are major prayer networks in other nations, too. The International House of Prayer in Kansas City has engaged in 24/7 prayer and worship since 1999. Their 2017 statistics show that there are 643 prayer houses connected to their ministry. Most of them are in the USA (509), some in Canada (22), and some in other nations (112).

Also in 1999, a prayer room was launched on the south coast of England. That ministry today, Prayer International, boasts of over 14,000 prayer rooms. Most of them are in England, Canada, and the USA. Online, there is a 24/7 Prayer Directory for Houses of Prayer, Boiler Rooms, Prayer Furnaces and other 24/7 Prayer Ministries. In their last update, on October 22, 2017, they cited 657 prayer houses. On their website, they write:

> "The last time we counted, that first prayer room had touched more than two million people in more than 10,000 prayer rooms in most denominations and more than half the nations on earth. Today we're still praying non-stop, night-and-day, from the slums of Delhi to a brewery in Missouri to a punk festival in Germany. Oh, and in churches and cathedrals too."

The Holy Spirit is impressing thousands of people to pray earnestly in these days. **1 Peter 4:7** says, *"The end of all things is at hand; therefore be serious and watchful in your prayers."* One of the activities that will mark true believers in the last days is that they will understand the urgency of prayer and engage in it. [If you would like more information on 24/7 Prayer Houses and prayer rooms, search the Internet for the International House of Prayer (Kansas City) and 24/7 Prayer International.]

Prepare for hard times

The time to prepare for a crisis is not when you are in it; it's before it comes! When you expect a famine, you store food in advance. When you expect war, you buy ammunition and weapons. We need to prepare *now* for the coming difficult times by drawing close to Jesus, tuning our ears to the Holy Spirit's voice, and becoming very familiar with God's Word and His ways.

Romans 13:11-12 says, *"Knowing the time, that now it is high time to awake out of sleep; for now our salvation is nearer than when we first believed. The night is far spent, the day is at hand. Therefore let us cast off the works of darkness, and let us put on the armor of light."*

The signs of the Lord's soon return are visible *today*! We need to realize the seriousness of the hour in which we live. Conditions are changing so rapidly in the earth that by the time you read this book, these facts and figures may well be outdated. Many believers today are distracted by the pleasures and cares of this world and have become blind to the end-time signs around them. We need to wake up and invest in the things that will last for eternity!

"Now when these things begin to happen, look up and lift up your heads, because your redemption draws near" (**Luke 21:28**).

Chapter 3

RELEVANCE OF GOD'S WORD

"...this generation will by no means pass away till all these things are fulfilled. Heaven and earth will pass away, but My words will by no means pass away" (**Matt. 24:34-35**).

Everything Jesus said about His return and the days leading up to it *will* be fulfilled. Don't believe the teachings that life will get better and easier, and that we can continue to live in sin because grace abounds. We need to prepare to go through the coming difficult days, not coast through these next years in ease. Jesus promised tribulation; we can count on it.

All of Jesus' words are relevant for us *now* and for the future. We must study the Bible in order to know what is coming and how we can stay faithful in the challenging days ahead. We need to believe God's promises, and proclaim them over ourselves, others, cities, and nations.

Relationship with God's Word

God can speak to us from any verse or chapter if we will open His Word and invest time and energy in reading it. We need to approach the Bible humbly and expectantly, not casually or distracted. We must ponder God's Word and let it sink deeply into our souls and spirits. We need to write it on our hearts. In His Word, the Lord reveals who He is, what He does, what He loves, and what He hates. The Bible is the blueprint of His heart, mind, and will. Jesus is the living Word and expression of God, but it is largely through the *written Word* that we encounter the living Word.

If we do not have a deep relationship with the Bible, we will tend to have a shallow relationship with God and a distorted or incomplete knowledge of Him. As we study and meditate on God's Word, the Holy Spirit deepens our intimacy with the Lord and tells us what He is saying *now*.

God's Word magnified upon His name

"I will worship toward Your holy temple, and praise Your name for Your lovingkindness and Your truth; for You have magnified Your word above all Your name" (**Ps. 138:2**).

The last phrase of this verse is insightful in Hebrew. *Magnified* is the Hebrew word, **gadal**, which means to make great or excellent, to enlarge, and lift up. *Above* is the word **al**, which means above or upon. *Name* is the Hebrew word, **shem**, meaning position, character, and authority. Putting it all together, this phrase says: *You have exalted, and made great and excellent Your word upon all Your character, authority, and position.*

Upon is the correct English preposition. The psalmist is saying that what God says and commands is based on Who He is and His authority. God has magnified all that He says upon His character. He is gracious, so His words are gracious. He is merciful and faithful, so His written and spoken words are merciful and faithful. He is righteous, so His Word is righteous; it's established upon His character. *"You have magnified Your word* upon *all Your name."*

Pray God's word

"As the rain comes down, and the snow from heaven, and do not return there, but water the earth, and make it bring forth and bud, that it may give seed to the sower and bread to the eater, so shall My word be that goes forth from My mouth; it shall not return to Me void, but it shall accomplish what I please, and it shall prosper in the thing for which I sent it" (**Isa. 55:10-11**).

There is power in praying God's Word! If we discern God's heart for someone and pray the appropriate Scriptures, we are praying His will for that person or situation. When we use God's Word in speaking or praying, we are releasing His Word to accomplish what He pleases. His Word cannot be fruitless or barren; it *will* accomplish what He sends it to do!

When our hearts and minds are filled with the Word, it will be obvious in our prayer lives. We'll pray boldly in faith, declare God's goodness, confess His faithfulness, and pray relevant verses over our concerns. We'll pray from a place of strong faith and victory. Our prayers will not be hesitant, filled with unbelief or fear.

Obey for blessing

"This Book of the Law shall not depart from your mouth, but you shall meditate in it day and night, that you may observe to do according to all that is written in it. For then you will make your way prosperous, and then you will have good success" (**Josh. 1:8**).

We are to meditate in God's Word day and night *so that we can obey* what is written. If we do, we will be blessed in our relationships, businesses, and ministries. The Hebrew word translated as 'success' is **sakal**, which means to be prudent. So, if we meditate on Scripture and obey it, we will be blessed with understanding, wisdom, and discretion.

Hebraic mindset

One reason some believers think they can read the Bible and have the *option* of obedience is because they have a Greek mindset rather than a Hebraic one. In the Hebraic worldview, the purpose of learning is to prepare for a life of obedience and service in knowing God. The Torah – the five books of Moses – was given by God as instruction to His people on how to live. Like their forefathers before them, the Jewish people are to study God's Word in order to live it. Understanding alone is not enough; *learning requires response.*

The fundamental goal of Hebraic education is the building of disciples— the passing on of the teachings and instruction of God to His children so that they might revere and obey Him. The Greeks, however, sought knowledge for the sake of knowledge. They wanted information in order to accumulate knowledge and to appear wise.

We tend to have a Greek mindset in the West, but we *should* adopt the Hebraic mindset that God intends for His people. *Judaism* is the root of the Christian faith; believers in Jesus have been grafted into the *Jewish* tree! The Bible is theirs, the covenants are theirs, the adoption is theirs, the giving of the law was to them, the promises are for them, and the Messiah came through their lineage! Yet God, in His mercy, has allowed non-Jews to partake of it *all* and be reconciled to Him. Their Messiah is available to everyone; He is the *only* path to salvation!

Our culture as believers is to be Hebraic, not Greek. We are to read the Bible in order to know what to do and how to live; we should not read it just to accumulate knowledge. Evangelist D.L. Moody said, "The Bible was not given to increase our knowledge but to change our lives." If we are not obedient to what we read, we can read the Bible every day and yet never become more like Jesus. We need to let the Scriptures renew our minds and transform the way we speak, think, and live.

God's Word should not touch just the periphery of our lives; it should be the *center* of our lives. As our minds are renewed in the Word of God, we are changed. Pastor Charles Stanley wrote, "We are either in the process of resisting God's truth or in the process of being shaped and molded by His truth."

"All Scripture is given by inspiration of God, and is profitable for doctrine, for reproof, for correction, for instruction in righteousness, that the man of God may be complete, thoroughly equipped for every good work" **(2 Tim. 3:16-17)**.

Benefits of reading God's Word

• It will direct your steps, and give you vision for the future.
• It will equip you to defeat the enemy when he tempts or attacks you.
• It will cause your prayer life to be effective and powerful.
• It will increase your faith in God and faithfulness to God.
• It will warn you of things to come and prepare you to endure.
• It will give you understanding and wisdom with an eternal perspective.

Our knowledge of the Bible is not for us only, it is also for everyone who hears us. We need to ingest the Scriptures so that we know them well. We are to be a voice to our generation and the generations after us, so we *must* know the truth of His Word and be able to share it. We must give to others the warnings and promises that God has given us. Let's cherish God's Word, stand on it boldly, and invest the time necessary for it to become our foundation and wisdom.

Chapter 4

SAFEGUARDS AGAINST DECEPTION

"Now as He sat on the Mount of Olives, the disciples came to Him privately, saying, 'Tell us, when will these things be? And what will be the sign of Your coming, and of the end of the age?' And Jesus answered and said to them: 'Take heed that no one deceives you. For many will come in My name, saying, 'I am the Christ,' and will deceive many... Many false prophets will rise up and deceive many... For false christs and false prophets will rise and show great signs and wonders to deceive, if possible, even the elect'" (**Matt. 24:3-5, 11, 24**).

The first warning Jesus gave His disciples concerning the end of the age had to do with the increase of deception. Certainly, we are seeing this today! How gracious and merciful the Lord is to warn us so that we don't have to be caught off-guard by the rise of deceivers and deceptions.

The apostle John wrote, *"Beloved, do not believe every spirit, but test the spirits, whether they are of God; because many false prophets have gone out into the world"* (**1 John 4:1**). In our day, new religious movements are springing up all over the world, numbering in the tens of thousands. These humanistic religions deviate from traditional doctrines. Most of them are found in Asia and Africa. In the USA, there are at least 20,000 cults and forms of the occult at the time of this writing (2017).

"Now the Spirit expressly says that in latter times some will depart from the faith, giving heed to deceiving spirits and doctrines of demons" (**1 Tim. 4:1**). The increase of deception, deceiving spirits, and doctrines of demons are resulting in many believers becoming sidetracked from the faith. Some are leaving Christianity altogether. Jesus did not say that *some* will be deceived; He said *'many!'*

Deception in the church

Within the Church, there has been an increase of deception. Some Christian leaders have wrongly believed they were instructed by God to leave their spouse to marry someone else. Many have hidden addictions; some have left the ministry due to an addiction to pornography or other perversions.

15

Some leaders have twisted the Word of God to suit their desires for pleasure or wealth. Many believers who were previously consecrated to the Lord are now living in compromise and disobedience. There is a growing number of Christians in the West who have become passive and apathetic about their faith; some have rejected the faith altogether.

We need to humbly remember that not one of us is beyond deception. We would be wise to build safeguards into our lives *now* so that we can avoid being deceived in the future. All of these precautions will require our determined effort.

Know the truth

We must study and know God's Word so that we can recognize error. Ultimately, each of us is responsible for our own spiritual growth. **Hosea 4:6a** says, *"My people are destroyed for lack of knowledge." "My people have gone into captivity because they have no knowledge"* (**Isa. 5:13**).

"Be diligent to present yourself approved to God, a worker who does not need to be ashamed, rightly dividing the word of truth" (**2 Tim. 2:15**). "Rightly divide" was a tentmaker's term for cutting material in a straight line. If the pieces were not cut just right, they wouldn't fit together properly. Even so, it is easy to take one verse out of context and make it say something other than what was intended. A person who is skilled in "rightly dividing" God's Word knows how a verse or passage fits with another, so that the meaning is understood.

People who work in the U.S. Treasury Department can easily detect counterfeit bills. The $50 and $100 bills are printed on rare paper, which feels slightly different than other paper. These trained people handle and study authentic bills in order to detect counterfeit ones. In a similar way, only when we *"handle"* the Word of God regularly can we discern counterfeit teaching.

If you hear a new doctrine, study it carefully in the Bible yourself. Don't believe doctrine based solely on who taught it. Be discerning and humble. Even famed Bible teachers have been deceived. *"Evil men and imposters will grow worse and worse, deceiving and being deceived. But as for you, continue in the things which you have learned... You have known the holy Scriptures, which are able to make you wise for salvation through faith which is in Christ Jesus"* (**2 Tim. 3:13-15**).

16

Love the truth

"In the beginning was the Word, and the Word was with God, and the Word was God... And the Word became flesh and dwelt among us, and we beheld His glory, the glory as of the only begotten of the Father, full of grace and truth" (**John 1:1, 14**). We can't love Jesus and not love His Word. We need to anchor ourselves in the Word of God!

"Let no one deceive you by any means; for that Day will not come unless the falling away comes first, and the man of sin is revealed, the son of perdition... The coming of the lawless one is according to the working of Satan, with all power, signs, and lying wonders, and with all unrighteous deception among those who perish, because they did not receive the love of the truth, that they might be saved. And for this reason, God will send them strong delusion, that they should believe the lie, that they all may be condemned who did not believe the truth but had pleasure in unrighteousness" (**2 Thess. 2:3, 9-12**).

The antichrist will be very convincing as he shows signs and wonders. He'll be terribly evil, cruel, and powerful, especially as he opposes Israel and the Church, God's two covenant peoples. Because he will hate God, he will hate His people and determine to destroy them.

People who don't love the truth of salvation and God's Word, and choose the pleasures of unrighteousness will easily be deceived by the antichrist. Some are deceived even now by the spirit of antichrist that is in the world today. Because people reject the truth that can save them, God will give them over to delusion. They will believe the lies and face God's judgment.

Consider these words of warning about the antichrist: *"He causes all, both small and great, rich and poor, free and slave, to receive a mark on their right hand or on their foreheads, and that no one may buy or sell except one who has the mark or the name of the beast, or the number of his name... A third angel followed them, saying with a loud voice, "If anyone worships the beast and his image, and receives his mark on his forehead or on his hand, he shall also drink of the wine of the wrath of God, which is poured out full strength into the cup of His indignation. He shall be tormented with fire and brimstone in the presence of the holy angels and in the presence of the Lamb.*

And the smoke of their torment ascends forever and ever; and they have no rest day or night, who worship the beast and his image, and whoever receives the mark of his name" (**Rev. 13:16-17, 14:9-11**).

It is vital that we know the truth and walk carefully and sensitively with the Lord. Even now, some Bible teachers and pastors are saying it will be acceptable to take the mark of the beast in order to preserve his life and care for his family. But God has warned us *not* to take the mark, nor to worship the beast. We must worship and serve God *only*, even at the risk of losing our lives on earth.

We are not just to give mental assent to truth; we are to love it! We must love the truth of righteousness, sanctification, and holiness, and live lives that reflect these qualities! Those who endure the perilous times to come will be sober minded and keep God's commandments and the faith of Jesus, we're told in Revelation 14:12.

Live the truth

James 1:22 says, *"Be doers of the Word and not hearers only, deceiving yourselves."* If we hear God's Word but do not obey it, our disobedience will make us susceptible to deception. We need to know, love, and *obey* the Scriptures! Any deception we accept and embrace will open a door to more deception. We must remove deceit, lies, and hypocrisy from our lives. We need to live honestly and with integrity. King David said in **Psalm 26:11**, *"As for me, I will walk in my integrity; redeem me and be merciful to me."*

1 John 1:6-7 says, *"If we say that we have fellowship with Him, and walk in darkness, we lie and do not practice the truth. But if we walk in the light as He is in the light, we have fellowship with one another, and the blood of Jesus Christ His Son cleanses us from all sin."* Our fellowship with one another is determined by the degree of light in which we walk. We are to walk in the light *as He is in the light*, putting off all sin and selfishness.

It's important that we have close fellowship with believers in Jesus. The enemy targets loners. The western world promotes independence and self-sufficiency, which do not display kingdom character or culture. The words that should describe us in the faith are trust, harmony, commitment, unity, and cooperation.

We need to love, honor, and cherish one another. Authentic godly relationships are a safeguard against deception.

Fellowship with people of truth

The Scriptures contain admonitions for us concerning with whom we are to associate. We are to be with men of integrity, those who are not angered easily, and who have good morals. We are to offer the gospel to anyone and everyone, but our closest associations and friendships should be with like-minded people who hold tightly to the truth and hate hypocrisy.

In the last days when there are shortages of food and basic necessities (due to famines, earthquakes, and wicked leaders withholding food from civilians), many people will be asking for help. The extreme needs will create opportunities for dishonest organizations to collect charitable funds only for personal gain. Some will present themselves as men and women of God who are caring for the poor and the marginalized, but they are actually lining their own pockets with the hard-earned cash of well-meaning donors.

Walk circumspectly

"A good man...will guide his affairs with discretion" (**Ps. 112:5**). We need to steward our resources with wisdom and discretion so that we know when to give to the poor and those who ask for help. We would be wise to save money in these days when many people spend loosely. Guard carefully what has been entrusted to your care, whether that's knowledge, wisdom, resources, gifts, or finances. *"Guard what was committed to your trust..."* (**1 Tim. 6:20a**).

According to Ephesians 5:15, we are to walk circumspectly. We are not to be careless and easily beguiled; we must know when to give and when to withhold. Our finances, like everything we own, belong to the Lord, and it is His prerogative to indicate where they should go and to whom. We should check the fruit of those to whom we give and with whom we labor. Are they genuine godly people with good fruit to show for their labors? Are they using resources wisely and for the good of others? Are they seeking the kingdom of God and His righteousness *first*?

One of the gifts of the Holy Spirit we desperately need is the gift of discerning of spirits. We need to discern by what spirit people are motivated: an evil spirit, their human spirit, or the Spirit of God. How well do you know the people to whom you give? Are you responding to requests that you receive from strangers or casual acquaintances, or do you know the people and their ministries personally? There are now and there will continue to be many asking for financial help; it is wise to check the soil into which we are sowing. We must not give indiscriminately; we need to be wise, fear the Lord, and listen for His leading. Not all people are what they seem to be.

People who love God and others are sensitive to the needs around them and want to alleviate them if they can. They trust easily because they have (*finally!*) learned to trust the Lord. But too often, they so desire to help the poor, that they give generously without clear leading from God. Because they trust too quickly, they can be deceived. Jesus calls us to be harmless as doves, but wise as serpents. We can trust the Holy Spirit Who lives in us to direct us. We are not to be stingy or to hoard goods for ourselves with fear of the future, nor are we to disperse finances freely and wisely without giving considerable thought and prayer beforehand.

1 Timothy 6:17-19 says, *"Command those who are rich in this present age not to be haughty, nor to trust in uncertain riches but in the living God, who gives us richly all things to enjoy. Let them do good, that they be rich in good works, ready to give, willing to share, storing up for themselves a good foundation for the time to come, that they may lay hold on eternal life."*

The last phrase in verse 18 says in Greek, "willing to communicate." Paul is not repeating the same thoughts in the last half of that verse, such as: *ready to give and willing to share your riches…* He is saying: be ready to give, and be *willing to communicate*, which means to associate and fellowship with, to have companions and partners. So, we are to do good with our wealth, be ready to give generously, and be willing to partner with others, to fellowship and communicate with them. To do all of that will take time, but that's the way of God's kingdom.

Recognize God's leading

A couple gave money to a pastor for the care of orphans who built a business with the money, they discovered later.

20

He did good works, but he was also deceitful and greedy. Although they had served with him for a short time, they didn't know him *well enough*. They didn't know his heart, motives, and the lasting fruit of his ministry. They hoped to alleviate the suffering of the poor, but actually gave unwisely. They had seen warning signs, yet their desire to care for the orphans overwhelmed the evidence. So, they gave and hoped for the best.

If we want to build the kingdom of God in others and in the nations, we must hold our finances loosely, be ready to share them generously, *and* be willing to invest the time and energy necessary to fellowship with others so that we can invest wisely. We are to *co-labor* in the work of God's kingdom. If we partner with others whom we know well, we will store up for ourselves *"a good foundation for the time to come, that* [we] *may lay hold on eternal life."*

Be humble

We need to walk in forgiveness and humility as we love and live the truth. In his book, *Dynamics of Spiritual Deception*, Dr. Daniel Juster says, "The two most important sources of deception are the heart matters of pride and bitterness. They often go together."

1 Peter 5:5b-6 says, *"All of you be submissive to one another and be clothed with humility, for God resists the proud, but gives grace to the humble. Therefore humble yourselves under the mighty hand of God, that He may exalt you in due time."*

The apostle Paul wrote, *"Do not set your mind on high things, but associate with the humble. Do not be wise in your own opinion"* (**Rom. 12:16b**). Just like Jesus laid down His life for others, so we are called to lay down our lives for the good of others. Clothed with humility, we are to serve one another.

When we are humble, we realize there is still a lot that we don't know, so we study God's Word in order to *know* the truth. We listen when people speak to us, knowing we can learn from anyone. To be humble is to hate hypocrisy, live in the light, and be accountable to others. It's being willing to be transparent despite the consequences. Because we love the truth, we welcome instruction and correction. *"Listen to counsel and receive instruction, that you may be wise in your latter days"* (**Prov. 19:20**).

Summary

To guard against deception, we need to know the truth. Pastor Mike Bickle says, "We must know what God says or we'll embrace what the world says." We must "handle" the Word of God often so that we can detect counterfeit teaching. We study God's Word so we can discern truth from error. Since deception will increase, our discernment must increase.

We must love the truth—the Living Truth (Jesus), the written truth (the Bible), and spoken truth. We need to let the Lord and those we trust speak into our lives. *"Let the righteous strike me. It shall be a kindness. And let him rebuke me; it shall be as excellent oil..."* (**Ps. 141:5**).

We need to live the truth, to walk as children of light in goodness, righteousness, and justice. We must cultivate godly relationships and be accountable to one another. True accountability involves the high cost of openness and vulnerability, but it also provides a haven for rich fellowship and encouragement. It is a tremendous safeguard against developing character flaws, unhealthy relationships, and wrong priorities.

So, we associate with people of truth. We work with and support those who are faithful in how they handle fame and funds. We partner with people who walk in integrity and righteousness, who shun deceit and hypocrisy. If we will live like this, **Proverbs 31:25** will be true of us: *"Strength and dignity are her clothing and her position is strong and secure; she rejoices over the future, knowing that she and her family are ready for it!"*

Deception was a major concern for the first century Church. It was addressed in almost every New Testament letter. Today, we clearly see an increase of it. However, we need not fear being deceived if we will wisely build these safeguards into our lives.

Chapter 5

DANGEROUS TEACHINGS IN THE CHURCH

Many people today question the absolute truth of the Word of God. Some have embraced rationalism and relativism, believing there are no absolutes and that there are many ways to God and Heaven. Chuck Colson wrote, "The problem is that relativism provides no sure foundation for a safe and orderly society."

The Scriptures make it clear that there *are* absolutes, and that there is only *one* way to God—through Jesus Christ (Acts 4:10-12, John 14:6). Only the sinless Son of God could pay the penalty for our sin with His blood, and provide the means for us to be reconciled to a holy God.

Some of the deceptions believed today are not blatant lies; they are truths taken to an unhealthy extreme to the exclusion of balancing truths. When we focus on one truth and exclude other aspects of truth we err. Unbalanced teaching is affecting thousands in the Church today. Some embrace it out of ignorance and others enjoy it because they like new and thrilling bits of knowledge.

When teaching becomes unbalanced, it can cause damage. Believers who hear abuses of truth may shrink back from and even reject the truth behind it. The Apostle Paul taught "the whole counsel of God" (Acts 20:27)—a full presentation of truth. Below are some of the current teachings that can cause harm and prevent God's people from reaching maturity in their relationship with Him.

1. Hyper-Grace adherents believe and teach that once saved, a person can live any way he chooses and still receive the benefits of salvation. Because we're saved by faith and not by works (Eph. 2:8-9), they believe the way we live is unimportant. But in reality, we must continually align ourselves with God's truth and forsake sin. Jesus is returning for a holy Bride. So, we need to put off the old, carnal man and put on the new man of righteousness and truth. *"...Shall we continue in sin that grace may abound? Certainly not! How shall we who died to sin live any longer in it?"* (**Rom. 6:1-2**).

Jude wrote in his epistle that we are to contend earnestly for the faith because ungodly men, who turn the grace of God into licentiousness and deny the Lord, have crept into the community of faith (Jude 3-4). That is also true today. We need to subdue the flesh and live to righteousness!

2. The Holiness movement emphasizes outward holiness over inward purity. Conservative dress is often required for one to be right standing with God. For example, women may not cut their hair or wear slacks, makeup, or jewelry. In Matthew 23, Jesus said inward holiness is a greater priority than outward conformance to religious demands. *"The Lord does not see as man sees; for man looks at the outward appearance, but the Lord looks at the heart"* (**1 Sam. 16:7b**). However, modesty befitting men and women of God is *always* in order!

3. Neglecting repentance – Some evangelists have been and are mightily used by God to bring many sinners to Christ through their preaching of repentance and obedience to the gospel. So, how is it that in many churches today repentance is not preached? As believers, we should be living a *lifestyle of repentance* where we easily sense the Holy Spirit's conviction and turn from our sin toward righteousness. John the Baptist, Jesus, and Peter preached repentance (Matt. 3:1-2, 4:17; Acts 3:19); how dare we neglect this basic aspect of God's kingdom?

4. Hyper-Love is a teaching about the love of God while *not teaching on His holiness* and the need to repent from sin. When we focus on one attribute of God to the exclusion of His other attributes, our view of God is unbalanced. The apostle John, who wrote, "God is love," also said that those who practice sin are lawless and of the devil because sin is lawlessness (1 John 3:4-10). We need to preach God's love *and* His call on us to walk in holiness! *"As He who called you is holy, you also be holy in all your conduct"* (**1 Pet. 1:15**).

5. Hyper-Faith teachers emphasize faith for healing and convince believers that there will always be victory with little suffering or pain if they have faith. Yet Jesus not only healed the sick, He also said His disciples must take up their cross and follow Him. He said whoever loses his life for His sake will save it (Mark 8:34-35). The apostle Paul, who suffered much for the sake of the gospel, wrote **Romans 8:18**: *"For I consider that the sufferings of this present time are not worthy to be compared with the glory which shall be revealed in us."*

6. Prosperity preachers overemphasize verses that promise blessings and financial prosperity. This can produce believers who seek the blessings more than the Blesser. It can also produce false expectations in those who sow money into a ministry expecting a hundredfold return, which rarely happens on a purely financial level. We must beware of a "rights-centered" gospel that creates attitudes of entitlement while ignoring proper biblical stewardship. We also need to teach that true riches are found in knowing the Lord, not in material gain. Jesus even told us *not* to store riches on earth! *"Do not lay up for yourselves treasures on earth, where moth and rust destroy and where thieves break in and steal"* (**Matt. 6:19**).

7. Unbalanced Charismatics focus more on the gifts of the Holy Spirit than they do on the Word of God, character development, and holiness. They elevate spiritual experiences above the truth of Scripture. We need it all—the gifts of the Holy Spirit and God's Word and holiness! **Psalm 19:7-8** says, *"The law of the Lord is perfect, converting the soul; the testimony of the Lord is sure, making wise the simple. The statutes of the Lord are right, rejoicing the heart; the commandment of the Lord is pure, enlightening the eyes."*

8. Hyper-Rational people fear subjective spiritual experiences and manifestations. They depend on their intellect rather than the Holy Spirit. They believe God *only* speaks through His written Word, and may neglect prayer. They seem to worship the Bible more than the Lord. Jesus said it is possible to study the Scriptures without coming to Him (John 5:39-40).

George D. Watson wrote, "The true saints of God, who have clear heads and pure hearts, have in all generations had to walk between the two extremes of cold formality on the one side, and wild, ranting fanaticism on the other. Dead formality and the false fire of fanaticism are both Satan's counterfeits, and he does not care into which extreme the soul plunges."

9. Torah Observance and Hebrew Roots Movements. Under the Old Covenant, non-Jews who wanted to be part of the people of Israel had to convert to Judaism. By the Holy Spirit, this was changed in Acts 10 and 15, and restated in Acts 21: *"But concerning the Gentiles who believe, we have written and decided that they should observe no such thing, except that they should keep themselves from things offered to idols, from blood, from things strangled, and from sexual immorality"* (**Acts 21:25**).

25

Gentile believers are *free* to be circumcised, keep the feasts, keep kosher, and embrace all 613 laws identified in traditional Judaism. But, if we *compel* non-Jewish believers to do such things, we move into error. Many of the laws are impossible to keep today, such as laws for making sacrifices, laws for Levites and priests, laws for making war, and some laws that only apply to a Theocratic state.

Here are a few of the false teachings of Hebrew roots movements that are rejected by the mainstream of the Messianic Jewish movement. Some movements combine several of these errors.

Error #1: Gentile Christians are to keep the whole Law just like Jews. This error is called "One Law" and is justified by Numbers 15:16. Adherents to this try to explain away Acts 15 and Galatians. They claim that *all* believers are called to keep the Law. This is contrary to many New Testament texts and ends in partial replacement theology since there is no longer any distinctive calling for Jews. These people teach that Christians must strictly observe all the Biblical feast days and the Sabbath. Many people in Torah-observant circles are not Jewish. We could wonder why non-Jews are so eager to observe a law never intended for them.

Error #2: True Christians are the lost tribes of Israel. Some claim that true Christians are physical descendants of the scattered lost tribes, which led to their conversion to Messiah. They explain away all of the texts that state salvation is available to the nations, and that the One New Man is made up of Jew and Gentile (Ephesians 2).

Error #3: Christian holy day celebrations are pagan abominations. Three of the main Christian Feasts are a Christianization of Jewish Feasts: Passover is celebrated as the death of Yeshua/Jesus on Good Friday, Early First Fruits as the Resurrection, and Shavuot/Weeks as Pentecost. The assertion that the Christian versions are pagan is wrong. They celebrate the events of prophetic fulfillment in Jesus' life and ministry, and when the Holy Spirit was poured out on the gathered disciples.

These errors have brought division, confusion, and pain to Christians, Jews, and Jewish believers in Jesus. We need discernment to avoid mistaken Hebrew roots teachings, and to be enriched by those that are correct. (For more information, read the writings of Ron Cantor and Dr. Dan Juster, Messianic Jewish leaders.)

A belief that can cause problems is Replacement Theology, which teaches that God has rejected the Jews and replaced them with the Christian Church. It says the Jews are no longer His chosen people; they have no future and no calling in the plan of God, and claims that God's blessings are reserved for Christians. But Romans 9-11 makes it clear that God is still faithful to His first covenant people, the Jewish people.

Knowing He is faithful to His first covenant people assures us that He will be faithful to His second covenant people also. In speaking of God's election of the Jews, Paul wrote, *"The gifts and calling of God are irrevocable"* (**Rom. 11:29**).

Dangerous practices

Besides dangerous teachings, there are also some dangerous practices in the Church today. Here are a few: (1) believing prophetic words that do not line up with the Word of God, (2) seeking revelation from angels, and (3) going to the grave of a great man of God to call up his anointing.

We must "receive the love of the truth" (2 Thess. 2:9-10) from the Holy Spirit and be avid students of God's Word if we are to avoid these extreme teachings. We need to understand and teach the whole counsel of God so that those we teach are able to discern and avoid deception.

Chapter 6

FACING THE FUTURE WITHOUT FEAR

"You will hear of wars and rumors of wars. See that you are not troubled; for all these things must come to pass, but the end is not yet. For nation will rise against nation, and kingdom against kingdom. There will be famines, pestilences, and earthquakes in various places" (**Matt. 24:6-7**).

Jesus warned His disciples that they would face terrifying situations in the future. Their future is our present. Many people are already facing dire conditions, which will only increase. Every circumstance Jesus warned of is serious: wars, famines, pestilences, diseases, and earthquakes. All of these life-threatening situations can cause extreme anxiety.

Fear is one of the main weapons in the enemy's arsenal. He uses it to torment us. If he can make us fear anything other than God, he has won a victory! Although Jesus said that men's hearts would fail because of fear, He doesn't want that to be true of us. We need to resist fear and anxiety and ask the Lord to uproot them from our hearts.

Fear – a common problem

Famous people throughout history have suffered from fears and phobias. Napoleon was crippled by ailurophobia, an irrational fear of cats. Queen Elizabeth I was terrorized by anthophobia, an abnormal fear of flowers (she particularly feared roses). Billionaire Howard Hughes was almost incapacitated by mysophobia, a pathological fear of germs. Edgar Allen Poe and Harry Houdini suffered from claustrophobia. The father of psychoanalysis, Sigmund Freud, suffered from agoraphobia, a fear of crowds and public places.

We must overcome fear or we'll never reach our God-given potential. A key to overcoming fear is finding where it got a foothold in our thoughts and lives. If we don't take our thoughts captive, as we are commanded in 2 Cor. 10:5, they will take *us* captive! Strongholds of fear begin with thoughts (usually planted in our minds by the enemy) that lead to imaginations (picturing that thought coming true).

29

Courting the imagination will lead to a stronghold of fear. When we are tormented by fear, we need to ask the Holy Spirit if there is a root cause or an open door to close as we ask Him to deliver us.

Open doors to fear

Many fears begin with lies from the devil. Jesus called him the father of lies in John 8:44. Satan wants to handicap us with fear, so he says things like: "You will fail... God will forsake you... You will never please the Lord... Your loved ones will die in an accident."

He says we won't get the job we applied for, or won't get the bank loan we requested. He may say our spouse will abandon us or our child will be kidnapped. When tormenting thoughts or lies are suggested to our minds, we need to immediately resist them in Jesus' name, and quote God's Word and His promises that directly confront them.

Another entryway for fear is witnessing or experiencing a traumatic incident. When we experience trauma, the enemy can acquire a foothold into our lives making us vulnerable to a spirit of fear. If you have had or witnessed trauma, solicit prayer and seek God until you find freedom. Jesus can heal you and set you free so that you no longer live in the present in response to your past.

Years ago, a believer named Jane shared her testimony. A man had attacked her and beat her terribly. She was terrorized by that memory for years. After someone prayed with her for healing in her memories and emotions, she forgave the man who assaulted her and prayed for his salvation. She then renounced the spirit of fear. She didn't have immediate freedom from the torment, but the process of freedom had begun. She asked her friends and family members to keep praying for her for full healing. Today she is free from fear and whole in that area of her emotions.

Tormenting fears can harass anyone who has watched dark movies or intense thrillers. The rise in adrenalin and corresponding anxiety a person experiences while watching a horror movie can open the door to a spirit of fear.

Some fears have generational roots. The spirits of fear can be transferred from generation to generation. What each person fears may differ, but the generational sin and stronghold of fear can be passed down.

We met with Sam, a man with panic attacks. His grandfather was a fearful man, and his father worried constantly. Fear was part of Sam's natural inheritance. He didn't suffer from irrational fear until his child was severely hurt. From then on, he was bombarded with anxiety and panic. The fear that was resident yet dormant in his spiritual DNA was activated. In prayer, Sam confessed the fear and worry of his forefathers and his own sin of anxiety. He asked the Lord to cleanse his bloodline with the blood of Jesus and to remove the fear factor from his DNA. He went on to resist fear, and to meditate on verses about trusting God to secure his freedom.

Another open door for fear is guilt. Guilt leads to fear of exposure and punishment. We fear disappointing people or being publicly humiliated. To cover our sin, we might lie. Then, we fear our lie will be discovered. We may worry that God will not forgive us, or that we are doomed to make the same mistake again.

Numerous girls and women suffer from fear because of having had an abortion. They fear that others will find out and judge or reject them, or that they will be sterile later. While living in Israel, we counseled some new immigrants who had had multiple abortions. Most of them had kept it a secret, living with fear, guilt, and shame. Once they confessed the sin, they were able to receive God's forgiveness and were set free from fear.

Attacks of fear

Fear attacks us in three primary areas: our faith, minds, and memory. Fear attacks our faith by robbing us of our trust in God. It attacks our minds by tempting us to expect the worst possible scenario. It attacks our memory by causing us to forget God's past faithfulness. We forget how He made provision for our healing and comfort us when we desperately needed divine help.

Faith, however, focuses on God's promises, power, and faithfulness. God is *always* reliable. He is with us in *every* circumstance; He has not abandoned us. We can experience peace if we will view our situations from His eternal perspective and entrust ourselves to Him.

1 John 4:18 says, *"There is no fear in love; but perfect love casts out fear because fear involves torment. But he who fears has not been made perfect in love."* As we receive God's love and love Him back, fear will lose its grip on us. Love will become a shield around our hearts that fear cannot penetrate.

Anxiety and worry

Anxiety is defined as a feeling of worry or nervousness. It usually relates to something with an uncertain outcome. It's the fear that something we dread might happen. Worry does not take away tomorrow's trouble, but it does rob us of today's strength. *"Worry wears a person down"* (**Prov. 12:25**). It is like a rocking chair—it gives us something to do in going back and forth, but we don't get anywhere!

Philippians 4:6-7 says, *"Be anxious for nothing, but in everything by prayer and supplication, with thanksgiving, let your requests be made known to God; and the peace of God, which surpasses all understanding will guard your hearts and minds through Christ Jesus."*

Supplication is prevailing prayer. It is praying until we have released the burden to the Lord *or* until the answer comes. We need to invest the time and energy necessary to pray until we reach a place of release and victory.

Anxiety causes disease

In 2008, we visited Reuven's sister who was suffering from cancer. We tried to talk about spiritual things with her, but she wasn't receptive. When we left her, Reuven was very burdened. He prayed for her, but not to a place of release. His burden was so heavy that he developed shingles. During that painful season, he learned to engage in a new dimension of prevailing prayer with thanksgiving. Although it was hard for him to give thanks, he pressed through to a place of victory. Five months later, we had the privilege of leading his sister to Jesus. She passed into Glory three weeks later.

If we follow God's instructions in Philippians 4:6, God will bless us with peace. *"If you do this, you will experience God's peace, which is far more wonderful than the human mind can understand. His peace will guard your heart and mind as you live in Christ Jesus"* (**Phil. 4:7**, NLB).

What a precious, powerful promise: a peace that guards our heart, thoughts, and emotions! When we've met the conditions of prevailing prayer and thanksgiving, God will give us His gift of peace, which will guard our hearts and minds.

Thoughts produce emotions

"...Whatever things are true, whatever things are noble, whatever things are just, whatever things are pure, whatever things are lovely, whatever things are of good report, if there is any virtue and if there is anything praiseworthy—meditate on these things" **(Phil. 4:8)**.

What you think about determines how you feel. If you question that, try to get angry without first having angry thoughts, or to feel sad without first having sad thoughts. You can't do it. To experience an emotion, you must first have a thought that produces it.

When we think about what is good and excellent and refuse to dwell on what is upsetting, our minds will be at peace! When we renew our minds in God's Word and think about Him, His peace will be our inheritance. *"You will keep him in perfect peace, whose mind is stayed on You, because he trusts in You"* **(Isa. 26:3)**.

No matter what happens in the months and years to come, we need to keep looking at Jesus! We need to keep hoping and trusting in Him. Even in dire circumstances, the Lord says to us: *"Fear not, for I am with you; be not dismayed, for I am your God. I will strengthen you, yes, I will help you, I will uphold you with My righteous right hand"* **(Isa. 41:10)**.

Chapter 7

INCREASE OF PERSECUTION

"For nation will rise against nation, and kingdom against kingdom. And there will be famines, pestilences, and earthquakes in various places. All these are the beginning of sorrows. Then they will deliver you up to tribulation and kill you, and you will be hated by all nations for My name's sake. But he who endures to the end shall be saved" (**Matt. 24:7-9, 13**).

In this last century, there were more Christian martyrs than in all preceding centuries combined. Over 119 million were killed for their faith. In this century, the death toll continues to rise. In 2015, there were more martyrs for Jesus than any other year. In 25 years of chronicling and ranking the restrictions on religious freedom experienced by Christians worldwide, Open Doors researchers identified 2016 as the "worst year yet," said Jeremy Weber in *Christianity Today* (January 11, 2017 issue).

"Persecution rose globally again for the third year in a row, indicating how volatile the situation has become," stated Open Doors. "Countries in South and Southeast Asia rapidly rose to unprecedented levels and now rank among such violent areas as the Middle East and Sub-Saharan Africa."

The findings and trends noted by Open Doors are glaring:

• About 215 million Christians experience high, very high, or extreme persecution.
• North Korea remains the most dangerous place to be a Christian (for 14 straight years).
• The total number of persecution incidents in the top 50 most dangerous countries increased, revealing the persecution of Christians worldwide as a rising trend.
• The most violent is Pakistan, which rose to number four on the list for a level of violence exceeding even northern Nigeria.
• Murders of Christians in Nigeria increased by more than 62 percent.
• The worst increase is found in Mali, Africa, which moved up the most places on the list from number 44 to number 32.
• Asia is a new center of concern, with persecution rising sharply in Laos, Bangladesh, and Bhutan. Sri Lanka joined the list for the first time.

Evangelist Franklin Graham highlighted the hardships faced by 215 million believers in a May 2017 summit on persecuted Christians. While acts of violence against followers of Christ often occur in Muslim-dominated countries, persecution is also rampant in supposedly democratic societies, he said. In an article written in *USA Today*, Graham cited data from Open Doors and Pew Research Center indicating that 75 percent of the world's population lives in places with severe religious restrictions.

The cost of following Jesus

Seldom is teaching on suffering or persecution included in the training of new believers in western countries, but it is spoken of freely and frequently where it's illegal to convert to Christianity. Muslims know they may be killed if they convert; orthodox Jews know they might be cut out of their inheritance and treated as dead by families; the Chinese know that prison and hard labor may await them if they love Jesus.

In America and other western affluent nations, believers tend to look at the benefits of believing in Jesus more than at the cost of surrender to Him. Persecution is not a popular topic of discussion. Seldom is it preached from their pulpits. In fact, it is more common to hear sermons on prosperity and blessing than to hear about suffering.

This has not been good for the shallow, self-centered Church in the West. God's people need to be told that suffering is part of our inheritance in God's kingdom. Jesus said in **Matthew 10:22**, *"And you will be hated by all for My name's sake."* Paul said in **2 Timothy 3:12**, *"All who desire to live godly in Christ Jesus will suffer persecution."* People who live worldly and carnal lives may not suffer much persecution, but those who desire to live godly lives will.

Persecution follows godliness

If you allow the Holy Spirit to transform you into Jesus' likeness, you will be persecuted. If you walk in the character of God's kingdom and in the power of the Holy Spirit, you will manifest the same nature as Jesus, and you *will* experience conflict. This lifestyle makes you radically different from the rest of the world and will evoke a negative response!

Jesus prayed to His Father prior to His arrest, saying: *"I have given them Your word; and the world has hated them because they are not of the world, just as I am not of the world"* (**John 17:14**). Speaking to His followers in **John 15:18,** Jesus said: *"If the world hates you, know that it hated Me before it hated you."*

Believers will be hated in most every nation prior to Jesus' return. Animosity will turn into rage in the near future. Many will be hunted and killed for Jesus' sake, but their love for Him will be so consuming that they will be fearless in the face of martyrdom.

Work persecution into your future

A pastor who goes regularly to China to minister to the Underground Church asked the pastors how they cope with arrests and imprisonment. They said, "We mentally work prison into our future. Then when we are arrested, we are not surprised." Like them, we need to understand and accept that persecution is an aspect of normal Christianity so that when we experience it, we will not be shaken. Jesus said, *"Blessed are those who are persecuted for righteousness' sake, for theirs is the kingdom of heaven"* (**Matt. 5:10**). In the four gospels, six times Jesus said: *"He who saves his life will lose it, and he who loses his life will find, save, and preserve it for eternal life."*

Some of the early apostles considered persecution a tremendous honor (Acts 5:40-41). They rejoiced to be counted worthy to suffer for Jesus' name. Although it pains God when His people are tortured or imprisoned, it gratifies Him that people are seeing His Son reflected in them. Joni Eareckson Tada says, "God permits what He hates to accomplish what He loves." Throughout the centuries, many people have come to faith in Jesus as a result of seeing Him revealed in His persecuted people.

The blessing of persecution

Harlan Popov was imprisoned for his faith in Bulgaria for over 13 years (1948-61). In his book, *Tortured for His Faith,* he told what happened to the Church when the Communists persecuted them:

"The suffering purified the church and united the believers in a wonderful spirit of brotherly love such as must have existed in the early church. There were no nominal or "lukewarm" believers.

It made no sense to be a half-hearted Christian when the price for faith was so great. There came a spiritual depth and richness in Christ I had never seen in the times before, when we were free. Everyone was forced to "count the cost" and decide if serving Christ was worth the suffering. To the great regret of the Communists, this was the healthiest thing they could have done for the church, for the insincere gave up but the true Christians became aware of what Christ meant to them and became more dedicated than ever before."

An unprepared heart

"He who received the seed on stony places, this is he who hears the word and immediately receives it with joy; yet he has no root in himself, but endures only for a while. For when tribulation or persecution arises because of the word, immediately he stumbles." (**Matt. 13:20-21**).

A stony heart is unprepared for persecution or suffering. People with hard hearts receive the Word readily, but because their hearts are not pliable and soft, they stumble when trials or persecutions come. They are happy with God's Word until it causes them pain. As long as it is convenient to walk with God, they will. But when things get difficult, they become offended and resist Him.

Tim Keller wrote, "If God allowed a Perfect Man to suffer terribly, why should we think that something like that could never happen to us?" If our hearts are hard and unprepared to be faithful in tribulation, it is likely that we will falter under persecution.

More than conquerors

"Who shall separate us from the love of Christ? Shall tribulation, distress, persecution, famine, peril, nakedness, or sword? As it is written: 'For Your sake we are killed all day long; we are accounted as sheep for the slaughter.' Yet in all these things we are more than conquerors through Him who loved us. For I am persuaded that neither death nor life, nor angels nor principalities nor powers, nor things present nor things to come, nor height nor depth, nor any other created thing, shall be able to separate us from the love of God which is in Christ Jesus our Lord" (**Rom. 8:35-39**).

We may be persecuted for righteousness, but that can't separate us from God's love. The Greek word translated as "more than conquerors" is **hupernikao**, which means to overwhelmingly conquer, to win more than an ordinary victory. Even while suffering, through Jesus we can be super-victorious!

Persecuted believers want Jesus to be seen in them. Because their chief goal is the salvation of others, what people do to them is irrelevant. They look at persecution only as an inconvenience or as an opportunity to die to self. They consider it an honor.

The cross

Jesus could have viewed the cross one of two ways: as torment and agony, or as a necessary and painful part in accomplishing His Father's will—the redemption of mankind. He chose the latter: *"He endured the cross for the joy set before Him"* (**Heb. 12:2b**). We have the same option: we can see our cross experiences (including persecution) as pain and agony to avoid, or we can see them as a necessary part of accomplishing the Father's will for us and others.

We read in Luke 23:33-34, that *while suffering* on the cross, Jesus said, *"Father, forgive them..."* Jesus forgave *during* the persecution. He pardoned the evil against Him before His horrific trial was even over! He forgave *while* on the cross in excruciating pain! He forgave so fully that once He was resurrected, He never once mentioned the sinful deeds of those who betrayed or crucified Him.

The Lord appoints sufferings for us, too. Have we let the cross have its full way in our lives? Have we died to ourselves through it, and risen to new life in Jesus? If the Lord has decreed suffering and tragedy for us, it was not to leave us there. It was to invite us to resurrection. Jesus has made available to us the possibility of living *above* the cruelty of men! We can emerge from our pain and death in victory for *His* glory and honor. We must fully forgive those who have wronged us *even while we are suffering*. Like Jesus, we must forgive *while* on the cross!

Jesus knew God's nature; He knew even while suffering that His Father was good, kind, and trustworthy. In that harsh place of agony, to Whom did Jesus commend Himself?

To *His Father,* the One who willed the cross for Him, the One Who allowed the whipping, mocking, and crucifixion. He commended His soul to the One Who chose His suffering and death. Why would He do that? *Because He knew Him.*

Do we know the Father like that? When we suffer, do we trust God to work it out for our good? When we are ridiculed and rejected, are we still anchored in His love? When we lose what is precious to us, do we say like Job, *"Though He slay me, yet will I trust Him"* (**Job 13:15a**)? Can we be fearless in the face of death as our Lord was?

Jesus showed us how to suffer, die, and rise again in victory: *while suffering*, we forgive and release our debtors. *While dying*, we entrust ourselves into the hands of our faithful Father. *Once resurrected*, we live in victory and never speak badly of those who caused our pain. That is the essence of a life of resurrection, the highest order of Christian living.

God allows suffering for *our* profit—that we might share His holiness. Suffering is an invitation to greater intimacy with Jesus. It yields a great depth of camaraderie with Him. When we experience persecution, we can know that *God has appointed us to it* for our good and His glory. His grace and presence are with us; He has not forsaken us.

The key to enduring

If personal comfort is our objective and we have no desire to inconvenience ourselves for the sake of others, then we will not be able to see the purpose in persecution because we have no joy set before us (their salvation or the strengthening of their faith). But if we long to see people enter the kingdom of God and walk faithfully and courageously with Him, we will willingly suffer persecution as a part of that process.

Whether we are suffering for our faith now or not, we *always* need to pray for people who are. **Hebrews 13:3** instructs us: *"Remember the prisoners as if chained with them – those who are mistreated – since you yourselves are in the Body also."* Open Doors Founder Brother Andrew says, "Our prayers can go where we cannot… there are no borders, no prison walls, no doors that are closed to us when we pray."

When we suffer, we should not focus only on the end of the suffering, but on His salvation that will be revealed through it. There are many blessings and benefits associated with suffering for Jesus. Let's not fear the pain, but instead, pray that we will be faithful in the midst of it. Instead of allowing difficulties or pressures to separate us from the Lord, let's use them as levers to press us closer to Him! With His grace, let's prove ourselves faithful to Jesus, and worthy to bear His name and glory. It is safe for us to commend ourselves into our Father's loving hands.

Jesus said, *"Blessed are you when they revile and persecute you, and say all kinds of evil against you falsely for My sake. Rejoice and be exceedingly glad, for great is your reward in heaven, for so they persecuted the prophets who were before you"* (**Matt. 5:11-12**).

Chapter 8

ESCALATION OF OFFENSE

"The disciples came to Him saying, 'Tell us, when will these things be? What will be the sign of Your coming, and of the end of the age?'... Then they will deliver you up to tribulation and kill you, and you will be hated by all nations for My name's sake. Then many will be offended, will betray one another, and will hate one another" (**Matt. 24:3, 9-10**).

In the Last Days, there will be an increase of giving and taking offense. Already, there is a destructive spirit of offense that is rising fast and running rampant throughout the Church. Many believers are offended over small issues. Satan wants to divide us in this hour of church history when it's essential that we unite on our common beliefs.

We have opportunities every day to be offended or to cause offense. To avoid this, we must protect our hearts with strong love for Jesus and for others. If offense is allowed to germinate, it will give birth to betrayal and hatred. Offense separates and destroys relationships between family members, friends, and co-workers. It causes people to leave churches, places of employment, marriages, and mission fields. Offense sets a person up for deception, and is the first step toward a cold, unresponsive heart. The sad truth is that the love of many believers is already growing cold, just as Jesus predicted in Matthew 24:12.

The word, offense, is the Greek word **skandalon**, which is the name of the part of the trap the bait is set on to lure an animal. *Vine's Dictionary* says offense is a hindrance or a stumbling block. When we offend others, we cause them to stumble. The *American Dictionary* says to offend is to cause anger, resentment, or hurt feelings. *"A brother offended is harder to be won than a strong city, and their contentions are like the bars of a castle"* (**Prov. 18:19**). *"Good sense makes one slow to anger, and it is his glory to overlook an offense"* (**Prov. 19:11**).

Ways to recognize the offended

How do you know when you are dealing with offended people? Here are seven easy ways to recognize them.

1. They complain about what people do or say to them—or don't do or say. They complain about the way others behave. Basically, they complain most of the time.

2. They are insecure and seek attention. They don't feel safe or secure in who they are, so they attack others to make them feel better about themselves. They demand attention, believing that attention equals love.

3. They pity themselves and feel victimized. They hope someone will take up their offense and give them special treatment because of the injustice they have endured.

4. They blame others for their emotions and circumstances. They don't take responsibility for their own feelings. They are easily angered.

5. They spread strife. They won't go to the one who offended them before they tell others what was done to them. They engage in gossip, slander, and sow discord.

6. They are negative and judge others. They believe the worst rather than the best of them.

7. They avoid reconciliation and will not respond to requests for it. They will avoid or ignore the other party and refuse to communicate for clarity. They refuse to forgive.

Causing offense

"It is impossible that no offenses should come, but woe to him through whom they do come! It would be better for him if a millstone were hung around his neck, and he were thrown into the sea, than that he should offend one of these little ones. Take heed to yourselves! If your brother sins against you, rebuke him; and if he repents, forgive him. If he sins against you seven times in a day, and seven times in a day returns to you, saying, 'I repent,' you shall forgive him" (**Luke 17:1-4**).

A millstone is the rolling, heavy stone on an olive press that crushes the olives, thus releasing the oil. Jesus said it is better to have this heavy stone hung around your neck and to be thrown into the sea than for you to offend someone precious to God.

In these verses, Jesus mentions two areas of offense: causing offense and being offended. He assures us that offenses will certainly come, but we dare not be the one who causes them!

There will always be difficult people, those who do not fit in or get along well with others. The admonition here is: don't *you* be that one! Don't *you* be the one to cause friction, be irritable, complain or criticize. Don't *you* be the one with an independent spirit, who doesn't function well on the team, who is rude or stubborn. Don't *you* be the one who controls or manipulates others.

Have you ever wondered why Jesus picked Judas? Jesus let Judas be in His inner circle although He was difficult and rebellious. Judas was critical (of Mary with the alabaster vial), a thief (he took money from the money box), and independent (he betrayed Jesus alone). He was not a team player. A benefit of having Judas as a disciple, though, was that he surfaced the sin and bad attitudes in the others. He exposed their hearts and motives.

Difficult people bring out the worst in us. They irritate and frustrate us. Actually, they show us our true selves. As we see our selfishness and intolerance, we realize our need to change. It's good for us to have difficult people around us—although we'd like to pray them out.

You might have a difficult person in your family or your inner circle. Just make sure *you* are not the offensive one. It's natural that there will be offenses, even in the Body of Christ. But don't *you* be the Judas! **Romans 14:13b** says, *"...let us resolve this, not to put a stumbling block or a cause to fall in a brother's way."*

There may be times we offend by taking a stand for what is right. Jesus offended people with truth and did not apologize for it. In order to keep from compromising the truth, we may not be able to avoid upsetting others. If that's why we offend, we must be like Jesus and willingly suffer the consequences.

Being offended

You may be offended and hurt by believers, leaders, and loved ones. Jesus said, *"Be careful, take heed..."* Watch out for unforgiveness! It can mature into bitterness that will defile you and others! Don't let offense lodge in your heart, take root, and spread its poison.

One of our hardest tasks is to keep our hearts free from offense. **Proverbs 4:23** says, *"Guard your heart with all diligence, for out of it spring the issues of life."*

When we refuse to forgive, we make ourselves vulnerable to attacks from the enemy because we are in direct disobedience to God. If we yield to bitterness and blame, we are in danger of a spiritual decline that may include lust and a desire for the world and the evil in it. If the enemy can detour us through offense, he might be able to prevent us from fulfilling God's purposes for our lives.

The enemy's strategy is to weaken our love. When we are offended by the sins and weaknesses that we see in others, we are guilty of lovelessness. Dudley Hall wrote, "Not every offense is intended nor is it personal. But because of our rejection, it is easy to find offense where none exists." If Satan can separate us from one another, he can deceive us more easily and rob us of joy. **1 John 4:20-21** says, *"If someone says, 'I love God,' and hates his brother, he is a liar; for he who does not love his brother whom he has seen, how can he love God whom he has not seen? This commandment we have from Him: that he who loves God must love his brother also."*

We say, "Lord, I love You" and He asks, "Do you love My people?" Our offenses toward each other offend *Him*! He's drawn by our worship but repelled by the lack of love and acceptance He sees in us. Unforgiveness is the bait of Satan to destroy our relationships, health, and spiritual vitality. We need to remember God's mercy toward us and give that same mercy to others.

Author and Pastor Francis Frangipane says,

> "In our modern era we have a different version of Christianity than that which Christ founded in the first century. Our version secures a hope in the afterlife but does little to change us in the present. We are as easily offended, unloving, and divisive as those who do not know the Lord. We marvel at what Jesus accomplished at Calvary, but we shrink from what He desires to fulfill in us. We desire His blessings but not His backbone."

46

Second hand offense

Maybe someone you love was wounded, overlooked, or slighted while selflessly serving God and His people. Be careful not to be offended at the injustices *others* have endured. You could stand it if it were you suffering, but you can't stand to see those you love hurt or mistreated.

Perhaps in your bitterness, you have developed distance between yourself and others. You may love the Lord but dislike His people. You feel torn between your love for God and your disdain of those He has chosen. Know that when you are frustrated by believers and close your heart to *them*, you actually close your heart to the Lord! None of us can afford that.

Unfulfilled expectations

A common cause of offense is unfulfilled expectations. We were created to find security in God alone, not in marriage or friendship. When the Lord becomes our source of peace and joy, our wellbeing is defined by our awareness of His love. When we put our confidence in Him, we can live more comfortably with the people around us. Instead of burdening them with unrealistic expectations, we can appreciate them with no strings attached.

Expectations can blind us to the efforts people *are* making and cause us to be disappointed and offended when they fail to measure up. Jesus said when we are offended we are to point out the sin, let the person apologize, and then forgive and be reconciled. When we forgive in our hearts but don't try to restore the relationship, we usually don't trust that person easily again. As a result, the relationship becomes shallow and superficial. God *always* wants reconciliation and restoration… *always!*

It's dangerous to hold onto offense for a long time. As we defend ourselves and blame others, our hearts grow cold. We justify ourselves instead of forgiving and seeking reconciliation. The anger and blame we carry develop roots of bitterness that choke the life of God in us.

An offense toward God

"Which of you, having a servant plowing or tending sheep, will say to him when he has come in from the field, "Come at once and sit down to eat"?

Will he not rather say to him, "Prepare something for my supper, and gird yourself and serve me till I have eaten and drunk, and afterward you will eat and drink'? Does he thank that servant because he did the things that were commanded him? I think not. So likewise you, when you have done all those things you are commanded, say, "We are unprofitable servants. We have done what was our duty to do" (**Luke 17:7-10**).

These verses speak of a third area of offense—taking up an offense toward God. Jesus' words challenge what we believe: who is the Master and who is the servant? Are we to serve God or is He to serve us? Sadly, among some believers in affluent nations, there appears to be a strong belief that God exists to make our lives comfortable and happy; He is here for *us*.

The root of offense is pride and self-centeredness, which we clearly see when we take up an offense toward God. As disciples who delight to obey God's commands, we cannot make special claims upon Him merely because we have fulfilled our duty of obeying and serving Him.

Maybe you have been offended at God. You haven't liked His choices for you, you've been unhappy with His timing, or He hasn't answered your prayers as you hoped or expected. You may feel He's been too hard on you. Perhaps you thought you knew God's plan, but things didn't turn out as you thought they would. You might have been hurt and disappointed, maybe even angry.

Perhaps God has required something of you that has been difficult. Maybe He has allowed trials and suffering in your life that you've resented. So, you have built protective walls around your heart. You don't feel tender toward people as you once did, and you don't hear the Lord's voice easily.

Romans 8:28 tells us that God causes all things to work together for our good and His glory. It is for our good to be conformed to His image through whatever means He uses. He wants to share His holiness and glory with us. His end goal is always good!

Offense against God is increasing dramatically today. We must be resolved that there is a King over history Who knows exactly what He is doing. We can trust Him! We *must* trust Him!

Holy jealousy

God has a high calling on His people. He hasn't called us to ease and comfort; He has called us to be just like His Son, walking in the same love, victory, and anointing. To bring us to that point, He has to refine us to get the pride and selfishness out. He may put on us demands of obedience that seem stricter than what He requires of others. He may seem to let them do things He won't let us do. We must not allow ourselves to be offended by them or by God.

The Lord may let others be famous, but keep us in the background. He may let others work for Him and be praised for it, but have us work for Him in secret. Sometimes He will even let others get the credit for what *we* have done. We need to die to the need for recognition.

The Holy Spirit may guard us with a jealous love and rebuke us for words we say, feelings we have, or for wasting time. Other believers may not feel those same convictions. We must beware of comparing ourselves with them. God has a right to do as He pleases with His own. He doesn't have to explain His ways to us. He is God, and we are not!

To flow in God's power and anointing, we cannot hold onto offense. We need to walk in unity, worship and pray together with open hearts, and love one another. To be strong people of God in the Last Days, we cannot afford to allow sin in the camp. Only if we are obedient can we be victorious in battle. We need to obey **Ephesians 4:1b-3**: *"...walk worthy of the calling with which you were called, with all lowliness and gentleness, with longsuffering, bearing with one another in love, endeavoring to keep the unity of the Spirit in the bond of peace."*

Free from offense

Ask the Holy Spirit to search your heart for offense. List those you have offended, and make a plan to ask for forgiveness. Then determine not to offend anyone again; live honorably. Change the offensive ways you speak and behave. Don't be the Judas!

Make another list of people you need to forgive. Give to them the same mercy you require from God. Pray thoroughly through your list, forgiving each one from your heart. Humbly seek reconciliation and restoration as quickly as possible. Make restitution as needed; pay back with interest!

If you have been angry with God, ask His forgiveness with godly sorrow and true repentance. Apologize to Him for resisting His choices and will, and for not trusting His love and wisdom. Then choose to walk free from offense from now on, by God's grace.

Maintaining a heart of love and trust is vital for us if we are to walk faithfully as Jesus' disciples and reach spiritual maturity. We need to accept other believers with grace and mercy just as the Lord received us. We must walk carefully and humbly before the Lord. We need clean hearts before God so that our discernment is sharp. We must be unified with each other so that we can accomplish what God has called us to do *corporately*—especially as we move further into the Last Days when offense abounds all the more.

Chapter 9

WISDOM BEFORE ADVERSARIES

"Nation will rise against nation, and kingdom against kingdom. And there will be great earthquakes in various places, and famines and pestilences; and there will be fearful sights and great signs from heaven. But before all these things, they will lay their hands on you and persecute you, delivering you up to the synagogues and prisons. You will be brought before kings and rulers for My name's sake. But it will turn out for you as an occasion for testimony. Settle it in your hearts not to meditate beforehand on what you will answer; for I will give you a mouth and wisdom which all your adversaries will not be able to contradict or resist'" (**Luke 21:10-15**).

In order for us to have wisdom that our enemies cannot contradict or resist, we must have surrendered our ears and mouths to God *already* so that we are accustomed to hearing His voice and proclaiming His Word. We must have *already* adopted submissive attitudes, and be filled with His Spirit with the word of Christ dwelling richly within us (Col. 3:16).

Called to be God's mouthpiece

Years ago, Charles W. Colson wrote a book entitled, *Who will Speak for God?* That is still a relevant question. Who *will* speak for God? Who *can* speak for Him? Who knows His heart and His mind? Who is pure enough to be His mouthpiece? Actually, God wants *all* of us to speak for Him! We are all people of influence. We touch lives every day that we can impact for God's kingdom. To be a mouthpiece for the Almighty God is no light matter; it's an awesome privilege and responsibility!

There may come a time when we speak for Him before rulers and leaders. We might share of His love and salvation or give prophetic words to them from the Lord. *Now* is the time to *prepare* to speak for Him! We need to sharpen our spiritual hearing and discernment, walk closely with Him to know His heart and ways, and feed daily upon His written Word so that it becomes incarnate within us.

The biblical prophets are good examples of men and women who spoke for God. They were called to speak God's words to kings, cities, people, dry bones, and in numerous situations.

51

We'll look at a few of the prophets briefly, and consider some common sins of the tongue that we *must* repent of if we are to speak with God's wisdom. We must be *holy* in word and deed in order to be a spokesperson for our holy God.

Consider Isaiah

"In the year that King Uzziah died, I saw the Lord sitting on a throne, high and lifted up, and the train of His robe filled the temple. Above it stood seraphim; each one had six wings: with two he covered his face, with two he covered his feet, and with two he flew. One cried to another and said: "Holy, holy, holy is the Lord of hosts; the whole earth is full of His glory!" The posts of the door were shaken by the voice of him who cried out, and the house was filled with smoke" (**Isa. 6:1-4**).

Uzziah began well as a king. He initially sought God's will, but later, his heart was lifted up in pride. He offered incense on the altar, which was a privilege that belonged only to the priests. As a result, God struck him with leprosy, and he died a leper. His disease and death must have been difficult for Isaiah; the prophet and king were close friends.

Seeing the Lord on His throne and hearing the angels' worship Him, Isaiah was convicted of his sin. He realized he was far from God's standard of holiness. He said, *"Woe is me, for I am undone! Because I am a man of unclean lips, and I dwell in the midst of a people of unclean lips; for my eyes have seen the King, the Lord of hosts"* (**Isa. 6:5**).

Isaiah cried out in despair and anguish! His words in Hebrew denote, *"I am unraveled! I am coming apart at the seams! I am a man of unclean lips and I dwell in the midst of a people of unclean lips!"* The Hebrew word translated *unclean* is **tamay**. It means defiled, polluted, and contaminated. Isaiah was convicted of his most ungodly area—*his tongue.* This wasn't a problem unique to Isaiah. We *all* have problems with our tongues! **James 3:8** says, *"No man can tame the tongue. It is an unruly evil, full of deadly poison."*

"One of the seraphim flew to me, having in his hand a live coal which he had taken with the tongs from the altar. And he touched my mouth with it, and said: "Behold, this has touched your lips; your iniquity is taken away, and your sin purged" (**Isa. 6:6-7**).

The angel took a burning coal from the altar and touched Isaiah's lips with it. And the iniquity—his inherited tendency to speak unclean words—was taken away! God cleansed his lips and atoned for his sin.

"I heard the voice of the Lord, saying: "Whom shall I send, and who will go for Us?" Then I said, "Here am I! Send me" (**Isa. 6:8**). In response to being forgiven and cleansed, Isaiah submitted entirely to God's service. He said, **"Hineini,"** meaning, *"Here am I."* This does not mean, *"Here I am; I have something worthwhile to say."* It means: *"Here am I with no merit of my own. I am Your humble servant, available to do Your will."*

The cleansing process was necessary before Isaiah could fulfill the task God was giving him. In a similar way, before *we* can do what God has called *us* to do, we must be cleansed. Our inherited tendency to speak defiling words must be taken away, and our sin of unclean speaking must be covered. We need God to cleanse our lips and atone for our sin.

Undergoing purification is very painful, but we *must* endure it so that God Almighty can speak through us. If we are to stand before world leaders, we *must* be able to speak boldly and wisely under the unction of the Lord.

Consider Jeremiah

"...For Your sake I have suffered rebuke. Your words were found, and I ate them, and Your word was to me the joy and rejoicing of my heart; for I am called by Your name, O Lord God of hosts. I did not sit in the assembly of the mockers, nor did I rejoice; I sat alone because of Your hand, for You have filled me with indignation. Why is my pain perpetual and my wound incurable, which refuses to be healed? Will You surely be to me like an unreliable stream, as waters that fail? Thus says the Lord: "If you return, then I will bring you back; you shall stand before Me; if you take out the precious from the vile, you shall be as My mouth. Let them return to you, but you must not return to them" (**Jer. 15:15d-19**).

Jeremiah was expressing his dejection and misery to the Lord. He reminded God how he had loved His Word, and that he was alienated because of God's hand upon him. He complained impatiently; he was not humble before God as he had once been.

Let's look at each phrase in verse 19. God said to Jeremiah, *"If you return, I will bring you back; you shall stand before Me…"* It's as if God were saying, "If you will repent and return to the patient, humble release of your prophetic function, I will bring you back to your former position. If you repent of complaining and self-pity, I will use you to speak for Me again."

"You will stand before me." He was speaking of being blameless and thus able to minister to God and intercede for others. In other words, God was implying, "Jeremiah, if you get your heart right, I'll bring you back to a place of authority and influence before Me on behalf of others."

"If you take out the precious from the vile, you shall be as My mouth." The Lord was saying, "If you will separate what is precious (My words and truth) from what is vile (your bitter, impatient words of complaint), you shall be as My mouth. I will trust you to speak for Me."

"Let them return to you, but you must not return to them." God was saying, "Jeremiah, you are to influence others; do not let them influence you."

Speaking words of life

If we want to speak for God, we need to repent of all sins of speech (bitter and complaining words; criticism; slander and gossip; lying; crude and vulgar words), and yield our tongues to the Lord. We need to remove what is precious from what is worthless so that we can influence others for God's kingdom. We must be blameless before God. *"He who has My word, let him speak My word faithfully"* (**Jer. 23:28**).

Proverbs 10:11a says, *"The mouth of the righteous is a well of life."* If we will diligently pursue righteousness and a pure heart, our words will minister life rather than death. Jesus said, *"Out of the abundance of the heart the mouth speaks"* (**Matt. 12:34**). We must repent of all lust, fear, anger, and pride. We need to allow the Lord to heal the hurting places in our souls so that offenses and wounds do not fester into bitterness.

Our tongues have the power to bless and to curse, to heal and to wound, to encourage and to discourage. As the Lord's spokesmen, we must use our words to build people up. *"Let no corrupt word proceed out of your mouth, but what is good for necessary edification, that it may impart grace to the hearers"* (**Eph. 4:29**).

In **John 6:63** Jesus said, *"The words that I speak to you are spirit and they are life!"* As the Lord's disciples, *our* words should be inspired by the Holy Spirit and release life. If we will meditate on God's Word, what we say will be an overflow of His life within us. Learning to speak for the Lord *now* will enable us to speak for Him under pressure in the future.

If we want our words to carry the Lord's authority, our mouths must belong to Him. Jesus said, *"I have not spoken on My own authority; but the Father who sent Me gave Me a command, what I should say and what I should speak... Therefore, whatever I speak, just as the Father has told Me, so I speak."* (**John 12:49-50**).

Consider Jonah

"Now the word of the Lord came to Jonah the son of Amittai, saying, 'Arise, go to Nineveh, that great city, and cry out against it; for their wickedness has come up before Me.' But Jonah arose to flee to Tarshish from the presence of the Lord. He went down to Joppa, and found a ship going to Tarshish; so he paid the fare, and went down into it, to go with them to Tarshish from the presence of the Lord" (**Jonah 1:1-3**).

When God's word came to Jonah, what was his response? He ran! He didn't want to be God's spokesman! Just like Jonah, we always pay a price when we flee God's presence, unwilling to speak for Him. The Lord might not release us from our situation and recruit someone else; He might just make our lives miserable until we submit to His call!

After three days in the great fish, Jonah was ready to obey God. *"Now the word of the Lord came to Jonah the second time, saying, 'Arise, go to Nineveh... and preach to it the message that I tell you.' So Jonah arose and went to Nineveh, according to the word of the Lord"* (**Jonah 3:1-3a**).

The word of the Lord came to Jonah a second time. This time, he delivered God's message to the Assyrians, but he didn't preach with compassion. Jonah had God's Word, but he didn't have God's heart.

We can be a chosen mouthpiece for God, but to really please Him, we need a heart of compassion. We need to love our enemies. Only God's character and nature within us will sustain His anointing upon us.

There have been many men and women of God who were gifted and called but did not have the character necessary to sustain those gifts. Many succumbed to sin and compromise. Some fell into immorality. Several left the ministry; a few even left the faith.

Don't be like Jonah who maintained his anger toward God and his prejudice against the Assyrians. In Jonah 4, we read that Jonah pitied a plant that was temporal while God pitied a city of eternal souls.

Prepare to speak for God

What do you pity? Does your heart break for what breaks God's heart? Are you, like God, unwilling that any should perish? That is what it will take for you to be ready to speak for Him in front of persecutors and ungodly rulers. If you are afraid and unwilling to share your faith now (in a free nation or when facing minor persecution), how will you ever share your faith when under pressure and threat of imprisonment or death?

Do you know the Holy Spirit's voice well enough to hear Him in a crisis? Are you willing to pay the price to become His mouthpiece so that when you stand before leaders, you will be able to speak with authority and wisdom? Do you know His Word well enough to speak it boldly? Evangelist Reinhard Bonnke said, "The Holy Spirit told me, 'My Word in your mouth is just as powerful as My Word in My mouth.' The power is in the Word of God."

Maybe you would say like Isaiah, *"Woe is me, for I am a man/woman of unclean lips."* If so, confess that to the Lord. Repent of the wrong use of your tongue and lips. Confess all words of criticism, complaint, slander, and other sins of the tongue. Ask the Lord to cleanse your lips and purge all ungodliness from them. Submit to His purifying process so that you can speak for Him!

Grow in your knowledge of and love for God so that you will have a heart of compassion to speak for Him. Invest time in reading, studying, and memorizing His Word. Meditate deeply on it so that you are filled with His wisdom. If you do, you will be able to stand before rulers in peace. You can trust that God will *"give you a mouth and wisdom which all your adversaries will not be able to contradict or resist"* (**Luke 21:15**).

Chapter 10

GROWTH OF BETRAYAL AND HATRED

"Then they will deliver you up to tribulation and kill you, and you will be hated by all nations for My name's sake... Many will be offended, will betray one another, and will hate one another" (**Matt. 24:9-10**).

In the coming days of tribulation, hatred will increase dramatically! Some believers have already felt animosity because of their faith; they know the pain of it. The Lord warns us in Matthew 24 that it will get much worse. Part of the high cost of following Jesus is being rejected and hated by those who resist Him.

In **Luke 21:16**, Jesus said, *"You will be betrayed even by parents and brothers, relatives and friends; and they will send some of you to your death. And you will be hated by all for My name's sake."* Those who betray believers are not always staunch enemies; some are relatives and friends. Many people today are already betraying people with whom they were in covenant relationship.

Some betrayers even walked with Jesus at one time, but when faced with severe hardship or persecution, they chose to deny Him. Some family members have turned in parents, siblings, and other believers to save themselves or to get revenge for the persecution they endured.

The pain of betrayal

Even though the Lord Jesus warned us about betrayal and hatred, it is still shocking and crushing when it happens to us. In western nations, we have not yet come under severe persecution, but some of us *have* experienced betrayal and were devastated by it. The infidelity of a spouse, a broken confidence, or deception by a spiritual leader or loved one can severely wound us.

Betrayal can cause chest pain and shock, leaving its victim numb and empty inside. It can produce chaos in the mind, rob a person of rest, and kill the appetite. It damages the soul. If allowed to fester and simmer, the hurt can mature into bitterness, and evoke hatred and an evil desire for revenge.

Death is tragic, but betrayal is like a living death because the offender is still alive and often present in the victim's life. The damage in hearts and minds from betrayal can be permanent unless the Lord heals it. Usually that relationship cannot be restored.

We need to ask the Lord to heal us from all pain of betrayal. It is likely that we will face more betrayals and hatred in the coming days. If we still carry pain from old wounds of betrayal, how will we ever weather new ones? If we do not deal effectively with the pain we have suffered in past broken relationships, the devil will use that pain to derail us and tempt us to be bitter and angry with God.

Breaking covenant

The National Secular Society in the USA offers certificates to atheists who want to revoke their water baptism and break the covenant they have with God. They estimate that in the years between 2012–2017, over 100,000 people downloaded the documents of renunciation from their website.

In these Last Days, tens of thousands of people are already turning away from the Lord and are vulnerable to the temptation of betraying Christians with whom they once had fellowship. As betrayal increases in the earth, we must resist all temptation to deceive or betray anyone. We must especially resist the temptation to deny the Lord.

Faithful to God's people

Besides loving God with all of our hearts, we are also to love our covenant partners: spouses, family members, and the Body of Christ. Because we have cut covenant with God, we are to express covenant kindness and love with all believers and dear friends with whom we are committed.

The Apostle Paul gives us these instructions in **Romans 15:5-7**: *"Now may the God of patience and comfort grant you to be like-minded toward one another, according to Christ Jesus, that you may with one mind and one mouth glorify the God and Father of our Lord Jesus Christ. Therefore receive one another, just as Christ also received us, to the glory of God."*

To walk with one another in unity, we must humbly accept each other despite differences and weaknesses. We are *called* to unity, so we must work at it patiently and gently, forbearing with one another in love.

Faithful within marriage

"... the Lord has been witness between you and the wife of your youth, with whom you have dealt treacherously; yet she is your companion and your wife by covenant. But did He not make them one, having a remnant of the Spirit? Why one? He seeks godly offspring. Therefore take heed to your spirit, and let none deal treacherously with the wife of his youth. 'The Lord God of Israel says that He hates divorce, for it covers one's garment with violence,' says the Lord of hosts. 'Therefore take heed to your spirit, that you do not deal treacherously'" (**Mal. 2:14b-16**).

When God unites two people in marriage, He makes them *one*. He is so serious about this relationship, that when a person is unfaithful within marriage, God refuses their sacrifices and offerings. Today, many people betray their marriage covenants through extramarital affairs, pornography, lusting after other men or women, and emotional attachments with people other than their spouses (emotional adultery).

Flirting with others, carnal teasing, and allowing your heart to stray is playing with fire! Don't do it! Stay faithful to your spouse and walk in purity and integrity with the partners of others. *"Keep your heart with all diligence, for out of it spring the issues of life. Put away from you a deceitful mouth, and put perverse lips far from you. Let your eyes look straight ahead, and your eyelids look right before you. Ponder the path of your feet, and let all your ways be established. Do not turn to the right or the left; remove your foot from evil"* (**Prov. 4:23-27**).

Faithful to covenant friends

The Lord graciously gives us dear friends to walk through life with us; to these, we must be loyal. Just like David had Jonathan (1 Sam. 18:1-4), we may be blessed with a covenant brother or sister. If so, we must care for these relationships! We should pray with and for our friends, and make time to invest in them.

"A friend loves at all times, and a brother is born for adversity" (**Prov. 17:17**). True friends will be motivated by love in their actions, words, and choices. They will speak the truth in love even when it hurts; the wounds of a friend are faithful (Prov. 27:6). They will be available to comfort, help, and encourage in times of need or trouble.

The betrayal of Achitophel

In 2 Samuel 15:12, we read of Achitophel, who lived in the days of King David. His wisdom made him famous throughout Israel. David appointed him as one of his chief counselors. Later, Achitophel's loyalty to David shifted and went to David's rebellious son, Absalom. Achitophel betrayed David in helping Absalom take the throne; he even gave Absalom a plan for David's demise! What happened to Achitophel that changed him from being good to David to planning evil against him?

In 2 Samuel 23:34, we see that Achitophel had a son named Eliam, who was one of David's mighty men. Eliam had a daughter named Bathsheba (2 Sam. 11:3). One day, David saw Bathsheba bathing, lusted after her, and called for her. Their intimacy resulted in pregnancy. David tried to cover his sin by bringing her husband, Uriah, home from the battle to be with his wife. Uriah's loyalty to the king and to his comrades in war prevented him from being intimate with his wife. Finally, David plotted Uriah's death on the battlefield and took Bathsheba to be one of his wives.

How do you think Bathsheba's family felt about this? Achitophel was surely deeply offended and angry! David had impregnated his grand-daughter, had her righteous husband killed, and then his great-grandchild born to Bathsheba died as a result of God's judgment. David's betrayal of Eliam and Uriah resulted in Achitophel's betrayal of David! Betrayal begets betrayal.

Achitophel's name consists of two Hebrew words: **achi** (my brother) and **taphel** (foolish). It means "my brother, the fool." Achitophel moved from being wise to being foolish because he allowed his offense toward David to result in betrayal and hatred, which led to a plan to commit murder. In time, Achitophel took his own life.

God wants us to learn from Achitophel's mistake of taking up an offense on behalf of another. Forgiving a person for offending someone we love is usually harder than forgiving someone who offends *us*. We do not have the grace it takes to forgive a second-hand offense.

Handling betrayal

Achitophel apparently never prayed through his offense toward David. He did not confront him or initiate a conversation that could have resulted in repentance, forgiveness, and restoration. Had he confronted David about his betrayal and infidelity, it is possible he could have avoided becoming treacherous himself.

When we are offended, we need to confront the one who caused the offense. If we do not talk *to* them, we will begin to talk *about* them destructively. We will betray them, exposing their weaknesses and sins. It's a form of revenge to turn the hearts of others against the person who hurt us. We may not physically commit murder, but slanderous words can kill relationships and reputations. Giving into resentment and anger leads us down a dark path away from God into a dungeon of hatred.

Forgiveness is key

Jesus Christ understands the pain of betrayal. He was betrayed by one of His disciples and friends. Jesus forgave Judas, and He can help us forgive those who betray us. His mercy is enough for us if we are guilty of betrayal, and enough for us if we bear pain for having been betrayed. His blood is more than sufficient for all of our sin and the sin of others—even the sins of deception, betrayal, and revenge.

After asking for and receiving the Lord's forgiveness and cleansing, we must choose to walk uprightly, determined not to let the enemy get an advantage over us. We must avoid even a *hint* of disloyalty to anyone with whom we are in covenant. When we know and believe God's loyalty to us, we want to be loyal to Him and to others. Loyalty begets loyalty.

We need to seek healing and restoration from former betrayals. We can offer God's mercy with the Lord's strength. He will help us release the pain and will bind up the wounds in our hearts and emotions. **Psalm 147:3** says, *"He heals the brokenhearted and binds up their wounds."*

If we refuse to forgive, we may betray people ourselves in the future. Victims usually become victimizers, except for the grace of God.

After you pray through all the pain, bitterness, betrayal, and hatred (whether you were the innocent party or the guilty one), receive the Lord's healing comfort. Rest in His love. Thank Him for His mercy toward you.

Declare these words from Psalm 30: *"I will extol You, O Lord, for You have lifted me up, and have not let my foes rejoice over me. O Lord my God, I cried out to You, and You healed me... You have turned for me my mourning into dancing; You have put off my sackcloth and clothed me with gladness, to the end that my glory may sing praise to You and not be silent. O Lord my God, I will give thanks to You forever"* **(Ps. 30:1-2, 11-12)**.

Chapter 11

LAWLESSNESS AND COLD LOVE

"Then they will deliver you up to tribulation and kill you, and you will be hated by all nations for My name's sake. And then many will be offended, will betray one another, and will hate one another. Then many false prophets will rise up and deceive many. Because lawlessness will abound, the love of many will grow cold. But he who endures to the end shall be saved" (**Matt. 24:9-13**).

Offense, betrayal, rejection, hatred, false spiritual leaders, and deception… all of these will lead to lawlessness. As lawlessness and persecution increase, love for God and others will cool. People won't love as deeply as they used to, and commitments and covenants will be easily broken.

We are seeing an increase of lawlessness in the world today. It's obvious that the Day of the Lord is drawing closer. Idolatry of every kind is increasing, perversion is widespread, and anarchy is rampant. We have seen a marked increase of it in the USA in the last few years.

2 Timothy 3:1-5 says, *"But know this, that in the last days perilous times will come: for men will be lovers of themselves, lovers of money, boasters, proud, blasphemers, disobedient to parents, unthankful, unholy, unloving, unforgiving, slanderers, without self-control, brutal, despisers of good, traitors, headstrong, haughty, lovers of pleasure rather than lovers of God, having a form of godliness but denying its power. And from such people turn away!"*

Why is it so tempting today to love pleasure rather than God? Part of the reason is because we have so many pleasure options now. Decades ago, life was simpler and harder. People didn't have all the comforts and conveniences we have. Men worked the fields and cared for farm animals and machinery. They worked in factories. They came home tired and went to bed early. Women cooked, cleaned, and sewed for their families. Children and teenagers often worked in factories, fields, or mines. They didn't play video games or look at social media.

Life in the USA in 1906

Over a century ago, the average life expectancy was 47 years. The average wage was $0.22 per hour. The average worker made $200–$400 per year. A three-minute phone call from Denver to New York City cost $11.

Only 14 percent of the homes had a bathtub, and only eight percent had a telephone. More than 95 percent of all births took place at home. Most women only washed their hair once a month and used borax or egg yolks for shampoo. There was no Mother's Day or Father's Day. Iced tea and crossword puzzles had not been invented yet.

There were only 8,000 cars in the U.S. and only 144 miles of paved roads. The maximum speed limit in most cities was 10 mph. The population of Las Vegas, Nevada, was 30. Two out of every 10 adults were illiterate. Only six percent of all Americans graduated from high school.

How different life is today! We have a surplus of pleasures: TV, smart phones, computers, tablets, video games, hobbies, sports to play or watch, and toys for people of all ages. We still work hard, but we also play hard. Instead of seeking rest that restores, we run after amusements, which entertain but do not restore our souls.

It's not just the plethora of what is available today it's also that we in the West have grown soft. We're spoiled. We believe we *deserve* to be comfortable, to have more than enough to eat and wear. We believe it's our right to do what we want when we want to do it. We like to be in charge of our lives and of how we use our time. We have made what is a luxury in third world countries to be a necessity in our first world nations.

Pleasure or God?

If we compare the love of pleasure and the love of God, we see that the differences involve lordship and sacrifice, happiness versus holiness, and living for today versus living for eternity. Pleasure is something we can control; God cannot be controlled. Most pleasures can be obtained easily, but a love relationship with God requires effort, discipline, and sacrifice. Pleasure benefits us now; the benefits of loving God are mostly in the eternal future. Pleasure has a narcotic effect; it takes our minds off of our problems. Love for God reminds us of our responsibilities and gives us guidelines for solving problems.

Pleasure cooperates with pride. It makes us feel good when we perform well or look respectable or successful in the eyes of others. But when we love God, we lay aside our pride and self-centeredness. Loving God over pleasure is a choice we need to make often, because the choices for entertainment, pleasure, and comfort abound. Sadly, the part of our busy lives that is often relegated to a back position is our time *with* the Lord and our service *for* the Lord, both which refresh and restore us.

God doesn't deprive us of *all* pleasure. He provides good things for us to enjoy, but we need to keep a proper perspective. We are allowed to enjoy temporal things as long as our main focus is on eternal things. God blesses us so that we can *be* a blessing.

"Command those who are rich in this present age not to be haughty, nor to trust in uncertain riches but in the living God, who gives us richly all things to enjoy. Let them do good, that they be rich in good works, ready to give, willing to share, storing up for themselves a good foundation for the time to come, that they may lay hold on eternal life" **(1 Tim. 6:17-19).**

Moses had wealth, position, and status, but gave it all up for the Lord and for an eternal reward. *"By faith Moses... refused to be called the son of Pharaoh's daughter, choosing rather to suffer affliction with the people of God than to enjoy the passing pleasures of sin, esteeming the reproach of Christ greater riches than the treasures in Egypt; for he looked to the reward"* **(Heb. 11:24-26).**

Separate from the world

In the midst of increased lawlessness, betrayal and hatred, we must keep our hearts free from offense so that we can love the Lord. And in the midst of distractions, entertainment, indulging of appetites and idolatry, we must love God first and foremost. Surrounded by uncleanness, we must stay pure. Surrounded by unfaithfulness, we must stay faithful. As anarchy abounds, we must walk in quiet submission to authorities unless they command us to disobey the Lord.

Consider Jesus' prayer for His disciples in **John 17:14-18,** *"I have given them Your word; and the world has hated them because they are not of the world, just as I am not of the world. I do not pray that You should take them out of the world, but that You should keep them from the evil one.*

They are not of the world, just as I am not of the world. Sanctify them by Your truth. Your word is truth. As You sent Me into the world, I also have sent them into the world."

Jesus has sent us *into* the world, but we are not *of* the world. We are to penetrate the darkness with His light. We must be righteous so that His holiness is vindicated through our lives.

1 John 2:15-17 says, *"Do not love the world or the things in the world. If anyone loves the world, the love of the Father is not in him. For all that is in the world—the lust of the flesh, the lust of the eyes, and the pride of life—is not of the Father but is of the world. And the world is passing away, and the lust of it; but he who does the will of God abides forever."*

Some people think that worldliness refers to external behavior, that it has to do with the people we associate with, the places we go, and the activities we enjoy. But worldliness is also *internal* because it begins in the heart. It is characterized by three attitudes: (1) a *craving for physical pleasure*—a preoccupation with gratifying desires; (2) a *craving for what we see*—coveting things and bowing to the god of materialism; and (3) *pride in our appearance, achievements, and/or possessions*—an obsession with appearances or status. We may avoid worldly pleasures, and yet harbor worldly attitudes in our hearts.

But when the love of the Father is in us, it's obvious! We view people with compassion like He does. We are generous and humble; we control our appetites; we serve and sacrifice in order to be a blessing. We love sinners and spend time with them while maintaining a commitment to the values of God's kingdom.

Knowing that this evil world *will* end should motivate us to deny ourselves temporary pleasures in order to focus on the things that will last for eternity. We dare not let worldliness cool our passion for the Lord. We cannot have the Father's love in us and see with His eyes if our eyes are clouded, and our hearts are led astray by a love for the world.

Intimacy with Jesus

If we love the Lord and love others as Jesus does, we'll be able to maintain a sense of peace even while people around us are pressured and stressed.

We will be content with simple material possessions because we'll be focused on eternity. We will bear lasting fruit instead of wasting time on frivolous matters.

While David was in the wilderness hiding from King Saul, he wrote Psalm 63. In spite of the harshness of his environment and the difficult men who were his constant companions, his heart and mind were set on God. He wrote, *"You are my God. I seek You early! My soul thirsts for You, my flesh longs for You. I want to see Your power and glory! Your lovingkindness is better than life. I will bless you while I live; I will lift up my hands in Your name. My soul will be satisfied with You as with abundance! My mouth praises You with joyful lips"* (**Ps. 63:1-5**). How clearly and fervently David expressed his love to the Lord!

We must not be satisfied with less than intimacy with Jesus. If we love God and seek His glory like David did, we will find the grace to forgive those who hate or betray us. We'll have the ability to walk humbly and holy before God, even though the world around us is proud and perverse. We'll obey **Philippians 2:14-15**: *"Do all things without complaining and disputing, that you may become blameless and harmless, children of God without fault in the midst of a crooked and perverse generation, among whom you shine as lights in the world..."*

As the world becomes more wicked, may the Lord find us to be more righteous. That won't come easily. We must *choose* to love the Lord our God with all of our hearts, minds, souls, and strength... *far* more than we love pleasure!

Excel in love

We need to love the Lord's family unconditionally, sensitively, and persistently. This is the level of commitment and love we need in the Body of Christ. We need to stand together regardless of what is going on around us. If we truly love one another, being faithful will be easy.

When the people of this world see us unified and devoted to one another, they will believe that Jesus is the Messiah. We are His Body, chosen to express and reveal Him to the world. His love cannot easily reach others if our love has grown cold.

"And this I pray, that your love may abound still more and more in knowledge and all discernment" (**Phil. 1:9**). Lawlessness *will* abound and the love of many *will* grow cold, but let's not let it happen to us!

Chapter 12

THE GOSPEL OF THE KINGDOM

"And this gospel of the kingdom will be preached in all the world as a witness to all the nations, and then the end will come" (**Matt. 24:14**).

Today the gospel of the kingdom is being preached around the world in person, on the radio and television, and via the Internet. In the midst of great persecution, thousands are coming to Jesus in Saudi Arabia, Sudan, Eritrea, China, and in many other nations. The top five countries where the gospel is growing today are Nepal, Iran, Afghanistan, China, and Mongolia. Experts who track Christianity around the world say the place where faith in Jesus is growing the most is in the Islamic Republic of Iran.

The core message of the gospel of the kingdom is that there is a King coming to the earth to confront everything that rebels against Him and His reign. He will fill the earth with love and deliver His people from their enemies. The glory of the Lord will be revealed and all flesh shall see it together (Isa. 40:5). The gospel begins with repentance and the remission of sin (Luke 24:47). It makes available to believers the power of the Holy Spirit (Acts 1:8). *And* it acknowledges that the King is coming to rule over individual lives and nations. Jesus is the King of His kingdom and of the increase of His government and peace there will be no end (Isa. 9:6-7)!

Christ for All Nations (CfAN), with evangelists Reinhard Bonnke and Daniel Kolenda, reports that at the crusade in Lagos, Nigeria in November, 2017, they had 845,875 recorded salvation decisions. Each of these converts will be followed up so that they can be established in their new faith. Since 1987, in CfAN gospel crusades around the world, over 77,044,650 decision cards have been turned in (as of January, 2018). Millions are being swept into the kingdom of God in this generation! Reinhard Bonnke says, "No revival comes if we don't preach God's Word under the anointing of the Holy Spirit. If we only have the Great Commission or only the Holy Spirit, we have power without purpose, or purpose without power. It is a package deal that God honors."

Many Christian leaders believe and claim that the greatest harvest in the history of the world is taking place right now.

According to pastor and author Mike Bickle, prominent missions leaders claim that the gospel will be preached in all 12,000 ethnic groups by 2020. Referring to God's promise to pour out His Spirit on all flesh (Acts 2:17-21), the number of those that testify to the outpouring of the Holy Spirit in their lives today has grown in the last 100 years from about 1 million (1920) to 60 million (1970) to over 600 million (2017).

All are commanded to go

Disciples of Jesus around the world are answering the call "to go" into every nation to share the gospel. Some are called to local missions, others to foreign missions. What they have in common is that they have heard the call to go, and they are faithfully obeying. Jesus Christ commands us *all* to go!

Matt. 10:7 – *"As you **go**, preach, saying, 'The kingdom of heaven is at hand.'"*
Matt. 28:19 – *"**Go** and make disciples of every ethnic group in all the nations."*
Mark 5:19 – *"Jesus said to him, '**Go** home to your friends, and tell them what great things the Lord has done for you...' "*
Mark 16:15 – *"**Go** into all the world & preach the gospel to every creature."*
Luke 9:60   – *"Let the dead bury their own dead, but you **go** and preach the kingdom of God."*
John 15:16 – *"I appointed you that you should **go** and bear fruit..."*

We are to go everywhere – to our neighbors and to the nations. Henry Martyn, a missionary to India and Persia two centuries ago, said, "The Spirit of Jesus is behind the spirit of missions, and the nearer we get to Him the more intensely missionary we must become."

Praying Hyde

John Nelson Hyde, a native of Illinois, USA, was a missionary to India in the late 1800's. When he went, he was one of only five missionaries in a territory of nearly one million non-believers. In 1899, he began spending entire nights face down before God in deep prayer.

In a letter, Hyde wrote: *I have felt led to pray for others this winter as never before. I never before knew what it was to work all day and then pray all night before God for another. In college or at parties or at home, I used to keep such hours for myself or pleasure, and can I not do as much for God and souls?"*

70

John Hyde had a consuming burden for India. By 1908, he prayed that during the next year in India one person would be saved every day. That year, 365 people were converted, baptized, and publicly confessed Jesus as Savior. The next year, Hyde prayed more than 400 people into God's kingdom. Then he doubled his goal to two souls a day; 800 conversions were recorded that year. Hyde's passion for souls was unquenchable.

In 1910, those around Hyde marveled at his faith as they witnessed his passionate prayers. He would plead, *"Give me souls, oh God, or I die!"* John Hyde doubled his goal for the coming year to four souls a day. During the next 12 months, he ministered throughout India. By then he was known as "Praying Hyde," and his intercession was sought at revivals in Calcutta, Bombay, and other large cities. If on any day four people were not converted, Hyde said at night there would be such a weight on his heart that he could not eat or sleep until he had prayed through to victory. The number of new converts continued to grow.

In Calcutta, friends persuaded Hyde to see a doctor about his declining health. The years of travail in prayer had taken a toll. The medical doctor found that his heart had shifted out of its natural position on the left side of his chest to a place over on the right. It was unlike anything he had seen before. He warned Hyde that unless he got complete rest he would be dead in six months. But Praying Hyde lived for nearly two more years, long enough to see a wave of revival sweep through the whole of India.

Eyes for the harvest

"Jesus went about all the cities and villages, teaching in their synagogues, preaching the gospel of the kingdom, and healing every sickness and every disease among the people. But when He saw the multitudes, He was moved with compassion for them, because they were weary and scattered, like sheep having no shepherd. Then He said to His disciples, 'The harvest truly is plentiful, but the laborers are few. Therefore, pray the Lord of the harvest to send out laborers into His harvest.'" (**Matt. 9:35-38**).

Jesus was teaching, preaching, and healing in the Galilee, ministering to multitudes. He saw their needs and felt compassion. The phrase *"moved with compassion"* means that his stomach twisted with emotion. He saw that they were weary, harassed, and scattered with no one to care for them.

To see their souls neglected broke the Lord's heart. Jesus didn't just glance at the multitudes; He *saw* them with eyes of love and pity. He ached for their salvation. Sometimes we wait for a specific call before we engage in evangelism and ministry, and we look past the harvest right in front of us.

Do you see the people around you? Does your heart break for their needs? Do you feel sick knowing that they don't know Jesus and are headed into eternity without Him? Do you *really see them,* or are you too busy with your concerns and responsibilities? Ask the Lord to break your heart with what breaks His—the multitudes of people who don't know Him.

Having Jesus' heart

When you have an intimate relationship with Jesus, you will know His heart and purposes, and will share in His sufferings. We want Him to get alongside us in our pain, but are we willing to get alongside Him in His?

Jesus said to His men, *"The harvest is huge! The laborers are few. Pray the Lord of the harvest to send out laborers into His harvest!"* The word for "send out" in Greek speaks of an almost violent thrusting or hurling of laborers into harvest fields. We are to *beg* God to thrust laborers into His harvest fields. Rev. Andrew Murray wrote, "The number of missionaries on the field is entirely dependent on someone praying for it or about it!"

It is while we are praying that God's heart is birthed in us. As we pray for the lost, we may say, *"Here am I, Lord, send me. Give me souls or I die! Let me be a harvest worker."* Ask the Lord to put the nations in your heart! Know what is happening in the world so that you can pray intelligently. You might want to get a world map and pray over it. Author Oswald Chambers wrote, "When the Spirit of God comes into a man, He gives him a worldwide view."

Missionaries on our knees

A South African couple raised their four boys to pray every day for missionaries. Each morning, the six family members gathered together and prayed through their individual lists of 25 names. The mother said, "If we can't be missionaries on the field, at least we can be missionaries on our knees." That's true for all of us. If we cannot do mission work because of age or disability, we can pray for those who can.

We can pray for cities and nations to have a fresh move of God that results in many people surrendering to Him. We can beg God to thrust laborers into His harvest!

Jesus said, *"Do you not say, 'There are still four months and then comes the harvest?' Behold, I say to you, lift up your eyes and look at the fields, for they are already white for harvest!"* (**John 4:35**).

Jesus used a Hebrew idiom when He said, *"Do you not say, 'There are still four months and then comes the harvest'?"* That idiom means, 'There's time; there's no need to hurry.' But Jesus corrected their understanding by saying 'the fields are white *now*; the harvest is rotting on the vines! There isn't time to waste!

Vision for the lost

Jesus directed His disciples to fix their eyes upon what was most important to Him—reaching and saving the lost. That was always the center of His focus. We never read of Jesus being distracted by the conditions around Him. He didn't complain about the Roman government that oppressed His people, the Jews. He looked past the conflicts, issues, and horrors of His time, and fixed His eyes on the harvest.

As Jesus' disciples, we must always look beyond our circumstances and the mundane things that demand our attention so that we can focus on His top priority—winning the lost. We need to lift up our eyes beyond the struggles of life and see what God is looking at—the fields that are *white* for harvest. The heart of God is *ablaze* for the lost.

God knows the critical condition and desperate dilemma of the lost, and He *"...is not willing that any should perish, but that all should come to repentance"* (**2 Pet. 3:9**).

Is that your priority and focus? When you look at people at a sporting event or in a mall or crowded area, do you see the harvest? As you walk in your neighborhood or city, do you feel the Lord's burden that all might know Him? Author and Holocaust survivor Corrie Ten Boom wrote, "Soul-winning is a task and privilege from which no Christian is exempt. All are commissioned."

Rev. A.H. Strong said, "What are churches for, but to make missionaries? What is education for, but to train them? What is commerce for, but to carry them? What is money for, but to support them? What is life for, but to fulfill the purpose of missions—the enthroning of Jesus Christ in the hearts of men?"

God has given us His prosperity to perform His priority—the salvation of others. He wants everyone to know Him! How many believers today have the Father's provision without the Father's vision? They have His resources, but they don't have His burden for the lost. How many are blessed by God's generosity but don't use it to expand His kingdom?

Don't say, *"There's time. We still have four months before the harvest is ready."* Lift up your eyes and look at the fields! They are *already* white for harvest! Beg the Lord of the harvest to thrust out laborers into His harvest fields!

Robert Moffat, a Scottish missionary to Africa and father-in-law of David Livingstone (famous missionary to Africa), said, "We will have all eternity to celebrate our victories, but only one short hour before sunset to win them." Time is short. We need to reach people *now* with the good news of the kingdom of God!

GO!

Chapter 13

READY WHEN JESUS COMES

"And as it was in the days of Noah, so it will be also in the days of the Son of Man: they ate, they drank, they married wives, they were given in marriage, until the day that Noah entered the ark, and the flood came and destroyed them all. Likewise as it was also in the days of Lot: they ate, they drank, they bought, they sold, they planted, they built; but on the day that Lot went out of Sodom it rained fire and brimstone from heaven and destroyed them all. Even so will it be in the day when the Son of Man is revealed. Remember Lot's wife. Whoever seeks to save his life will lose it, and whoever loses his life will preserve it" (**Luke 17:26-30, 32-33**).

Jesus said the days of His return to earth would be like those of Noah's day. People will be enjoying relationships, looking forward to the future, unaware and unprepared for what is coming. They will have no idea that their lives are about to be radically changed by God's judgment. There will be no warning. Most people will be as surprised by Jesus' second coming as the people in Noah's day were by the torrential rains and flood.

The day of Jesus' second coming will also be like the days of Lot. People will be working, buying and selling, planting and building, indifferent to God and His will. They will be living for themselves and their pleasures. No warning will sound. Most people will be as shocked by Jesus' return as the people in Lot's day were by the unexpected destruction of Sodom.

The sins of Sodom

Genesis 19 recounts the story of God burning Sodom and Gomorrah with fire and brimstone (sulfate). The people of Sodom are condemned most often for sexual perversion, but that wasn't the only sin for which God judged them. **Ezekiel 16:49-50** says, *"Look, this was the iniquity of your sister Sodom: She and her daughter had pride, fullness of food, and abundance of idleness; neither did she strengthen the hand of the poor and needy. And they were haughty and committed abomination before Me; therefore I took them away as I saw fit."* Sodom was destroyed because of her pride, laziness, idleness, overeating, lack of concern for the poor and needy, and sexual abominations.

Are we guilty of any of these sins?

Are we proud? We show our pride when we are arrogant, argumentative, conceited, jealous, easily angered, self-centered, and stubborn.

Do we have "fullness of food?" Are we guilty of gluttony? Do we eat more than we need or should, thus yielding to the lusts of the flesh? Does our appetite control us?

What about idleness? Do we waste time, or are we intentional and strategic with our time and activities, knowing that Jesus is coming back soon? Are we guilty of slothfulness or do we work hard, even when no one is looking? Do we sacrificially serve others?

Are we strengthening the hands of the poor and needy? Are we helping them find work and emerge out of the cycle of poverty? Or do we ignore and neglect them? *"He who oppresses the poor reproaches his Maker, but he who honors Him has mercy on the needy"* (**Prov. 14:31**).

Are we guilty of illicit sexual conduct? Do we think we can do whatever we want and get away with it? There are numerous sexual abominations in our sex-crazed societies today, including homosexuality, adultery, bestiality, incest, pedophilia, and sex slavery. One of the most common and highly destructive sexual sins is viewing pornography. It is more addictive than heroin and literally damages the brain (for more information on this, see *The Conquer* DVD series).

If we are innocent of obvious sexual abominations, we may think we are doing well. But are we guilty of the other sins: pride, laziness, gluttony, and indifference to the needy? These sins may not be as abhorrent to us, but God judges them strongly.

Repent!

If we are guilty of the sins of Sodom, we need to repent! We need to live righteously! That means:

- Instead of being proud and arrogant, we are humble and teachable. We prefer others and work toward unity with one another.
- Instead of engaging in sexual sin, we live honorably. We're faithful in action, thought, and word to our Lord and our spouses. If we are single, we are chaste and devoted to the Lord.

- Instead of being gluttonous, we discipline our appetites; we avoid over-eating and resist fleshly lusts. We practice self-control. We fast regularly.
- Instead of ignoring the poor and needy, we care for them, generously giving to them as is appropriate. We help them find employment. We feel a personal responsibility toward the poor. We *are* our brother's keeper.
- Instead of being idle and lazy, we work hard; we're productive. We stay busy until Jesus comes, doing what He has called us to do. The preacher and commentator John Wesley said, "Leisure and I have parted company. I am resolved to be busy till I die."

We don't know *when* Jesus will return, but we do know that He's coming. We must be morally and spiritually ready, living as if He were returning in *our* day, *at this moment.* We must beware of becoming too attached to worldly things. We are called to be holy, set apart from this world.

Pray in faith

The theme of the parable in Luke 18:1-8 is that we are to pray continually with faith while waiting for God to answer. This parable is connected to Jesus' teaching on the days prior to His return. As we see evil increase around the world, our prayers should also increase and intensify. **Luke 18:7-8a** says, *"His elect cry out day and night to Him, and He bears long with them... He avenges them speedily."* It sounds like a paradox, but this is one of the ways of God: He *waits* while we cry out in prayer day and night. Then *suddenly* He answers. *Suddenly* He avenges us. *Suddenly* He heals or provides or gives us the guidance we seek. He waits... and then He acts quickly.

When Jesus comes, will He find us strong in faith, crying out to God day and night, standing firm in trust believing He *will* answer? Will He find us with our hearts engaged with His, and our eyes singly focused on Him?

In the parable in Luke 18, the widow was unjustly wronged and harassed by an enemy. She pleaded with the judge to avenge her. He became weary of her pleading and decided to act just to silence her. If godless judges respond to constant pressure, how much more will our loving Father respond to us? We know He loves us, and can be sure that He will hear and answer our cries.

Jesus is addressing the need to keep praying with faith in spite of delayed answers. There are times when God designs a delay in order to produce a specific work in us through the pain of unresolved suffering. We are to persistently pray until His work is complete in us and He answers. Crying out to God continually qualifies us to enter into His fuller purposes. To quit praying is to forfeit.

Even though God does not always answer quickly, He never waits too long. He waits as long as is necessary, but when the intended work is complete, He acts speedily. If you have been waiting a long time for God to answer certain prayers, keep praying! When God finally answers, you may be shocked at how quickly things change.

Trust in God alone

When God delays answering, it takes great faith to persevere in seeking Him *only*. Some believers falter in their faith, stop praying, and look to other sources for help. It is this that Jesus addresses when He says, *"When the Son of Man comes, will He really find faith on the earth?"* The question is not, will He find "saving faith" (people being saved), but will He find the kind of faith that insists on seeking God *especially* when answers are delayed? Will He find people that will keep praying until the solution comes?

To persist in prayer means we keep our requests continually before God as we live for Him every day, believing He *will* answer. God may delay responding, but His delays always have good reasons. As we pray boldly, we grow in godly character, faith, and hope. We ignore distractions, put away sin, and live focused, righteous lives before God.

Choices determine destiny

The Lord's second coming will be instantaneous. There will be no opportunity for last-minute repentance. The choices we make now *will* determine our destiny.

"As the days of Noah were, so also will the coming of the Son of Man be. As in the days before the flood, they were eating and drinking, marrying and giving in marriage, until the day that Noah entered the ark, and did not know until the flood came and took them all away, so also will the coming of the Son of Man be" (**Matt. 24:37-39**).

It is good that we don't know exactly when Jesus will return. If we knew the precise date, we might be tempted to be lazy or to compromise with the world. Or worse, we might plan to keep sinning and then turn to Jesus right before He arrives.

Remember: Heaven is not our only goal; knowing God *now* should be our determined purpose. God has prepared good works for us to do *here*. We have a destiny *here*. The Lord has a claim on our lives, and we must keep doing what He's called us to do until He takes us to Himself.

Repent and surrender

If you are guilty of one of the sins of Sodom (pride, sexual sin, laziness, gluttony, or ignoring the poor and needy), confess that to God and repent. Diligently take steps toward purity, assertive action, discipline in eating, and caring for the poor. Refuse to pamper your flesh; seek the crucified life instead. Repent of being easily distracted and addicted to comfort and the pleasures of this world. The Lord wants to conform you to Himself in *all* things. The best choice you can make is to surrender to His will.

Watch and pray

"For you yourselves know perfectly that the day of the Lord so comes as a thief in the night. For when they say, "Peace and safety!" then sudden destruction comes upon them, as labor pains upon a pregnant woman. And they shall not escape. But you, brethren, are not in darkness, so that this Day should overtake you as a thief. You are all sons of light and sons of the day. We are not of the night nor of darkness. Therefore let us not sleep, as others do, but let us watch and be sober" (**1 Thess. 5:2-6**).

Don't be caught sleeping when Jesus comes. Be alert and ready. If He is calling you to more intercession, obey Him! Prayer is hard work but worth it. The late revivalist Leonard Ravenhill wrote, "The prayer room of the church is the boiler room for its spiritual life." And Dr. Charles Spurgeon said, "I would rather teach one man to pray than 10 men to preach!"

When Jesus returns, may He find faith-filled people where *you* are, in *your* city, in *your* church, in *your* circle of friends, in *your* home who cry out to Him day and night, trusting Him with all their hearts—even in seasons of delayed answers.

"Watch therefore, for you do not know when the master of the house is coming—in the evening, at midnight, at the crowing of the rooster, or in the morning—lest, coming suddenly, he find you sleeping. And what I say to you, I say to all: Watch!" (**Mark 13:35-37**).

Chapter 14

RESPONSIBLE AND FAITHFUL SERVICE

"Who then is a faithful and wise servant, whom his master made ruler over his household, to give them food in due season? Blessed is that servant whom his master, when he comes, will find so doing. Assuredly, I say to you that he will make him ruler over all his goods" (**Matt. 24:45-47**).

God has given us all gifts and talents that we are to use for the benefit of others and for His glory. In Matthew 25, Jesus told a parable about the faithful discharge of responsibilities. He said that the wise employment of gifts and abilities entrusted to us results in our receiving more opportunities to serve. Mother Teresa of Calcutta, India said, "God has not called me to be successful; He's called me to be faithful."

The apostle Paul warns us not to neglect our God-given gifts in **1 Tim. 4:14a**: *"Do not neglect the gift that is in you, which was given to you by prophecy with the laying on of the hands of the eldership"* To neglect means to despise, disregard, or ignore. It is to refuse to decisively serve with our gifts. It is a serious thing to neglect what God has entrusted to us!

One reason we don't use our gifts is fear, or more literally, intimidation. Paul wrote, *"I remind you to stir up the gift of God which is in you through the laying on of my hands. For God has not given us a spirit of fear, but of power and of love and of a sound mind"* (**2 Tim. 1:6-7**). The spirit of intimidation is determined to keep us from doing what God has called us to do. We need to recognize this spirit so that we can deal with it effectively and fulfill God's call on our lives.

A spirit of intimidation

When a spirit of intimidation attacks you, you feel anxious, inadequate, and confused. The enemy plants thoughts of rejection and worthlessness in your mind. You wonder about God's call on you. You might feel discouraged and frustrated.

This spirit often attacks us after we have done a good work for the Lord to rob us of proper perspective. No matter how successful our service was, we might imagine failure. The stronger the intimidation, the more hopeless we feel.

81

Without spiritual discernment, we will focus only on our feelings and ignore the cause of those feelings. Since intimidation is a spirit, it cannot be fought on the level of the intellect or will. Having a positive mental attitude alone cannot overcome this spirit. Spiritual warfare is required.

The devil is the author of intimidation and fear. His goal is to control and limit us. He might whisper lies directly to us, or he may work through people. We need to strongly resist this spirit, while being gentle, firm, and wise in dealing with people who intimidate us.

1 John 4:17-18 says, *"Love has been perfected among us in this: that we may have boldness in the day of judgment; because as He is, so are we in this world. There is no fear in love; but perfect love casts out fear, because fear involves torment. He who fears has not been made perfect in love."*

Perfect love casts out fear because it focuses on God and others rather than on self. When we are willing to emerge out of our comfort zones in order to serve, we are maturing in love. We show that we are concerned for others' needs to be met and are willing to use our money, energy, and time to meet them. To reach out requires us to risk, which we are willing to do when we truly love.

Fear of man

William Gurnoil wrote, "We fear men so greatly because we fear God so little." When we fear man, we make every effort to avoid rejection and confrontation. We concentrate on pleasing others and protecting ourselves, which renders us ineffective in our service for God. Afraid of what man can do to us, we fail to consider what God can do if we disobey Him.

"Do not fear those who kill the body but cannot kill the soul. But rather fear Him who is able to destroy both soul and body in hell" (**Matt. 10:28**).

The root of fear is the love of self. When a person loves his life, he is intimidated by anything that threatens it. The pathway to freedom from intimidation is to fear the Lord. To fear God is to respect and glorify Him.

A person who fears God will not be afraid of man because he fears offending God. When we fear men we are more concerned with what they think than what the Lord thinks. We will offend the One we cannot see in order not to offend the one we can.

When we let fear dominate our hearts, we lose our peace and courage. We cannot focus on serving the Lord *and* pleasing people. Paul wrote, *"For do I now persuade men, or God? Or do I seek to please men? For if I still pleased men I would not be a bond-servant of Christ"* (**Gal. 1:10**).

Virtues for boldness

Holy boldness comes as we walk in the virtues found in 2 Timothy 1:7 – the power of the Holy Spirit, a love for God and others, and a sound mind that knows God's will. As we walk in the power of the Spirit and our God-given authority, we are authorized to do what Jesus did: preach repentance, heal the sick, and cast out demons. We are not only to preach the kingdom of God, we are also to demonstrate it in power.

When we love God and others above ourselves, we are eager to sacrificially serve. We are willing to lay down our lives and comfort for the sake of others. We employ the gifts the Lord has given us to minister to and bless people, even if naturally we prefer to stay in the shadows.

The Lord has given us a sound mind so that we can act with confidence. When we hear His voice, we grow in love with Him; we *want* to obey Him; our faith and courage increase; our minds are settled; our hearts are steadfast. We fear the Lord and are not shaken by the enemy's attempts to intimidate us.

The stronghold of intimidation

There are some actions you can take in order to break the stronghold of intimidation off of your life. After acting on the following four points, you can ask the Lord to awaken His gifts within you.

1) Pursue a pure heart before God. Repent of pride and the fear of man.
2) Forgive everyone who has intimidated you.
3) Confess the sin of yielding to intimidation and disobeying God.
4) Resist the spirit of fear and intimidation in Jesus' name (as often as necessary).

Prayer guideline

Abba Father, thank You for adopting me as Your child. Thank You for gifting me to serve You. Please forgive me for neglecting those gifts.

Holy Spirit, expose and remove any insecurities I have that have opened a door to a spirit of fear. Heal any wounds that cause me to want to please people over pleasing You. Set me free from the need for man's approval. Please meet my needs for love and acceptance.

I repent of pride, unbelief, and the fear of man. I repent of allowing people to control and intimidate me. I confess and renounce fear. I rebuke every spirit of fear, and command them to leave me in the name of Jesus Christ! I break the fear of man off of me in Jesus' name. I choose to submit to God. In every place where I have given in to fear, I take that ground back and give it to the Lord. King Jesus, sit on the throne of my heart and rule over me. I forgive everyone who has intimidated me in the past or is intimidating me now. Please bless them.

Father, awaken in me the gifts You have given me. Baptize me in Your love and power. Give me a sound mind. I ask for a greater release of the power of the Holy Spirit, more love for You and others, and an ability to hear Your voice and discern Your will. Thank You! In the name of Jesus, I pray, amen.

Rewards and regrets

On Judgment Day, there will be rewards and regrets. Jesus highlights this in the story in Matthew 25. He spoke of three servants who were given talents to invest for their master. The first two invested well and were rewarded; the third one buried his talent and was judged appropriately. The first two were willing to risk failure and invest. As a result the Master said, *"Well done, good and faithful servant"* (**Matt. 25:21**). The third servant said, *"I was afraid, and went and hid your talent in the ground"* (**Matt. 25:25**). He made a common and tragic mistake when it comes to giftedness: he failed to benefit the Master with his talent.

God wants us to live free from all intimidating fear. He wants us filled with a compelling love for Him infused with holy boldness. We must refuse to allow previous failures to hold us back. We are to responsibly use the spiritual gifts God has given us to build His Church and bless others. When Jesus returns, may He find us doing what He called and gifted us to do!

Chapter 15

ANOINTED WITH OIL

"The kingdom of heaven shall be likened to ten virgins who took their lamps and went out to meet the bridegroom. Now five of them were wise, and five were foolish. Those who were foolish took their lamps and took no oil with them, but the wise took oil in their vessels with their lamps. But while the bridegroom was delayed, they all slumbered and slept. At midnight a cry was heard: 'The bridegroom is coming; go out to meet him!' Then all those virgins arose and trimmed their lamps. And the foolish said to the wise, 'Give us some of your oil, for our lamps are going out.' But the wise answered, saying, 'No, lest there should not be enough for us and you; but go rather to those who sell, and buy for yourselves.' While they went to buy, the bridegroom came, and those who were ready went in with him to the wedding; and the door was shut. Afterward the other virgins came also, saying, 'Lord, Lord, open to us!' But he answered and said, 'Assuredly, I say to you, I do not know you.' Watch therefore, for you know neither the day nor the hour in which the Son of Man is coming" (**Matt 25:1-13**).

The ten women were *all* virgins, they *all* slept while waiting for the bridegroom, and they *all* awoke and trimmed their lamps when they heard he was coming. Where they differed was that some carried *extra* oil with them besides that which was in their lamps. The ones with the extra oil were ready to meet the bridegroom; the others ran out of oil and had to go buy more. The first five were welcomed to the wedding; the last five were not. The Lord said to them, *"Assuredly, I say to you, I do not know you."* How tragic it will be if we are not carrying extra oil when Jesus returns!

What does the oil in the lamps signify? There were a variety of uses for oil in ancient times; any one or most of them could be to what Jesus was referring. All of them carry a message for us today. Let's consider each of them and determine to carry the oil of His anointing until our beloved Bridegroom comes.

Oil used for light

A common use of oil was for light. Olive oil was put in small clay lamps holding a wick. When the wick (soaked in oil) was lit, the lamp would light up the room. *"You are the light of the world. A city set on a hill cannot be hidden. Nor do men light a lamp, and put it under a bushel, but on the lampstand; and it gives light to all who are in the house. Let your light so shine before men that they may see your good works, and glorify your Father who is in heaven"* (**Matt. 5:14-16**).

Ephesians 5:8 says, *"For you were once darkness, but now you are light in the Lord. Walk as children of light."* The Apostle Paul did not say, "You had some darkness and now you have some light." He said, *you were* and *you are*. Your basic nature is changed. You are not just called to stand up for what is righteous, you are called to *be* righteous. We need to allow the oil of the Holy Spirit *within* us to be the light all *around* us in this world, especially in the dark days ahead.

Matthew 5:15 tells us to not to hide or limit our light (it is to give light to *all* that are in the house). It is not the lampstand (vessel) that is important, but the lamp (Jesus). The Holy Spirit Who lives within us produces the oil for our lights to shine.

"For it is the God who commanded light to shine out of darkness, who has shone in our hearts to give the light of the knowledge of the glory of God in the face of Jesus Christ. We have this treasure in earthen vessels, that the excellence of the power may be of God and not of us" (**2 Cor. 4:7**).

The fresh oil of hospitality

Anointing with oil was part of good hospitality in ancient times. When people came to dinner, the host of the table would anoint their heads with perfumed oil, provide water for their feet to be washed, and kiss them on each cheek. The anointing showed favor and generosity.

We see the hospitality anointing in **Psalm 23:5**: *"He anoints my head with oil, my cup overflows."* When we sit at God's table, He anoints our heads with perfumed oil. We receive His generosity and favor and an overflow of His provision, which fills us with thanksgiving and joy!

It is *while we sit at His table* that He anoints our heads with oil. If we never relax and dine with Him in intimate fellowship, we will miss this anointing! Jesus might say to some of us as He did to the lukewarm church of Laodicea, *"Behold, I stand at the door and knock. If anyone hears My voice and opens the door, I will come in to him and dine with him, and he with Me"* (**Rev. 3:20**).

Jesus doesn't want just a quick snack with us; He wants to *dine* with us— to have a full meal with appetizers, numerous courses, desert, coffee, crackers and cheese, and chocolates! Jesus invites us to engage in rich, prolonged communion with Him. He has made *provision* for it; it is up to us to make *time* for fellowship with Him.

Psalm 92:10b says, *"I have been anointed with fresh oil."* We receive an anointing of fresh oil by devoting time and energy to prayer and worship. Fresh oil flows out of intimacy with the Lord in the secret place. If we will respond to the call to intimacy with our Bridegroom, we will have more than enough oil when He comes.

We need to sit more often and for longer periods of time with the Lord, the Host of His table. We need the fresh anointing that comes when we respond to His invitation to dine with Him. Too often we rush through our devotions instead of lingering in His presence. The more we fellowship with Jesus, the more oil we will accumulate.

Anointed for service

Anointing oil was used to set people and objects apart for God's service. Future leaders were anointed with oil for their work or ministries. When God chose to replace Saul, the king of Israel, He sent the prophet Samuel with oil to anoint David, who would be the next king.

"The Lord said to Samuel, 'How long will you mourn for Saul, seeing I have rejected him from reigning over Israel? Fill your horn with oil, and go; I am sending you to Jesse the Bethlehemite. For I have provided Myself a king among his sons.'... Samuel said to Jesse, 'Are all the young men here?' Then he said, 'There remains yet the youngest, and there he is, keeping the sheep.' And Samuel said to Jesse, 'Send and bring him. For we will not sit down till he comes here.'

So he sent and brought him in. Now he was ruddy, with bright eyes, and good-looking. And the Lord said, 'Arise, anoint him; for this is the one!' Then Samuel took the horn of oil and anointed him in the midst of his brothers; and the Spirit of the Lord came upon David from that day forward..." (**1 Sam. 16:1, 11-13**).

David's intimacy with the Lord while shepherding sheep in the fields prepared him for leadership. After David was anointed by Samuel, *"the Spirit of the Lord came upon David."* This fresh anointing brought favor, blessing, power, recognition, revelation, and insight by the Spirit of the Lord. It set David apart from all others. Evangelist Smith Wigglesworth said it well, "An uneducated man with God's anointing accomplishes far more for God than an educated man without it."

The priestly anointing

Jewish priests were anointed with the blood of a ram before they were anointed with oil. The blood was put on their right ears; they were to hear the Word of God *only*. The blood was put on their right thumbs; they were to rightly perform their duties as priests. And the blood was put on the big toe of their right foot, which meant they were to walk righteously. After being anointed with blood, they were anointed with special oil made out of specific ingredients.

In Jesus Christ, our King and great High Priest, royalty and priesthood come together. He has anointed us as kings *and* priests to God. Jesus *"loved us and washed us from our sins in His own blood, and has made us kings and priests to His God and Father..."* (**Rev. 1:5b-6**) We have been washed *all over* in the blood of the Lamb of God—not just anointed on our thumbs, toes, and ears. He has consecrated and commissioned us to do His work. So we hear the Word of God and speak it, we serve and do good works, and we walk in paths of righteousness.

"You, also, as living stones, are being built up a spiritual house, a holy priesthood, to offer up spiritual sacrifices acceptable to God through Jesus Christ. You are a chosen generation, a royal priesthood, a holy nation, His own special people, that you may proclaim the praises of Him who called you out of darkness into His marvelous light" (**1 Pet. 2:5, 9**).

As priests, we are to minister to God in worship and to stand before Him in intercession for others. He wants us to take a responsible and active role in His will being accomplished on earth. We are given power and authority through prayer because we are *seated with Christ in heavenly places* (**Eph. 2:6**). In the hidden place of intercession, God's priests carry a special portion of His presence. They walk in intense commitment, active faith, and Holy Spirit power. They maintain a disciplined and devoted prayer life.

To actualize the privilege and responsibility of priesthood, we must be holy, filled with God's Spirit, and endeavoring to overcome sin. We are to be so identified with Jesus that we are one with Him in His death, in His resurrection, and on His throne. We should express both the crucified life and the victorious life in our daily walk with God, enabling us to say like Paul, *"I have been crucified with Christ; it is no longer I who live, but Christ lives in me; and the life which I now live in the flesh I live by the faith of the Son of God, who loved me and gave Himself for me"* (**Gal. 2:20**).

Anointed for healing

Oil was and *is* used to anoint people for healing. Even before our salvation was purchased, Jesus' disciples used oil as they prayed for people for healing. *"And they cast out many demons, and anointed with oil many who were sick, and healed them"* (**Mark 6:13**).

The practice of anointing with oil is common in some churches today, but scarcely practiced in others. We need to remember that anointing with oil is a *biblical* thing to do; it's not just a denominational practice. **James 5:14** says, *"Is anyone among you sick? Let him call for the elders of the church, and let them pray over him, anointing him with oil in the name of the Lord."*

Along with using oil as we pray for the sick, our lives should be full of the oil of the Holy Spirit. Then, as we speak and interact with others, His healing grace will be released through us to them.

Extra oil

The five foolish virgins in Matthew 25 were called "foolish" because they did not take *extra* oil with them. They had only enough for each day. We are guilty of that when our devotional lives consist of just enough of the Word and prayer to make it through that one day.

We will need more than daily maintenance to be overcomers in the days ahead! The five wise virgins not only had oil in their lamps, they also carried extra oil with them. They were prepared for the unexpected delay of the Bridegroom.

In these days, we *must* carry extra oil. We need to receive the anointing by the Host while reclining at His table. We need a leadership anointing to obey God's call on us. We need the priestly-kingly anointing as people of prayer and worship; we must walk in the power of the Holy Spirit with spiritual authority. We need to carry a healing anointing with a strong sense of God's presence in our lives.

We dare not run out of oil. We can't depend on someone else's relationship with Jesus or another's anointing to carry us through the hard times ahead. We need to cultivate the oil of intimacy in *our* lives so that we can stand and withstand in the evil day. We must prepare *now* for the increasing spiritual conflict to come by investing in a deeper relationship with the Lord!

Gulf War I

We lived in Israel during the first Gulf War in 1991. We prepared for it as fully as we could. Reuven sealed the cracks in the walls of our small rented house against chemical weapons. We bought plastic sheeting and tape to seal the windows, electrical outlets, and doors. We had extra food, water, and emergency equipment. Yanit took a first aid and chemical warfare course, and we had rubber outfits and boots to protect us from possible nerve or mustard gases released on warheads from Iraq.

There were some who refused to prepare for the war. They didn't buy plastic sheeting and tape or seal a "safe room" in their home. So, when the war started, they panicked. One older woman frantically called for someone to tape her windows as she heard the warning sirens, but all tape had been sold out weeks before. She wildly tried to put on her gas mask, only to get it terribly entangled in her hair. She knew the Lord, but she wasn't prepared for the war. She didn't believe the warnings.

Heed the warnings! Increasingly difficult times *will* come! *And the time to prepare for war is not when it is upon us!* The time to prepare for Jesus' return is *not* at the last minute. We need to prepare now by accumulating extra oil in our hearts and lives!

Oil of intimacy

We need to invest the time necessary to cultivate the oil of intimacy. We must choose to seek God for fresh revelation, fresh understanding, and fresh anointing. The key word is *fresh*. What we have heard and known in the past may not sustain our faith in the coming season. We are entering escalating end-times warfare, and many will be deceived and fall away. Scores will not stand during the evil day.

As priests of the Lord, we need to find God in the secret place of prayer so that we can emerge with fresh oil and revelation to declare the Word of God without compromise. If we are faithful in the throne room before God, He will trust us to be His voice to people in the earth.

Author and preacher Tommy Tenney said, "The height of your revival will be the depth of your desire." In other words, you can have as much of God as you want and seek. Tommy also said, "Your hunger for God will take you places nothing else can." We need to seek personal revival! The best thing we can do sometimes is to lay aside our agendas and schedules and fall on our knees.

Linger in His presence

God desires a people who will linger in His presence, unconcerned with convenience. He is calling us to abandon our agenda for His agenda. Intimacy with Jesus will lead to our carrying His anointing and fragrance. Our hearts should reflect David's as expressed in **Psalm 27:4**, *"One thing I have desired of the Lord, that will I seek: that I may dwell in the house of the Lord all the days of my life, to behold the beauty of the Lord, and to inquire in His temple."*

We *must* embrace an authentic passion for the Lord's presence. The fragrance follows the oil. We are called to carry His fragrance, and it begins with intimacy and a lifestyle of lingering with Him. The world needs to encounter those who refuse to leave His presence, and therefore, carry His aroma. *"Now thanks be to God who always causes us to triumph in Christ and through us reveals the fragrance of His knowledge in every place. For we are to God a sweet fragrance of Christ among those who are saved and among those who perish"* (**2 Cor. 2:14-15**).

91

We need extra oil so that we can be a light in this dark world. **Philippians 2:15** says we are to be *"blameless and innocent, children of God without fault in the midst of a crooked and perverse generation, among whom we shine as lights in the world."*

If we will wisely accumulate oil in *this* season, we will be ready for the Bridegroom, even if He delays His coming! *"He who testifies to these things says, 'Surely I am coming quickly.' Amen. Even so, come, Lord Jesus!"* (**Rev. 22:20**).

Chapter 16

RISE IN LOVE OF SELF

"Know this, that in the last days perilous times will come: for men will be lovers of themselves, lovers of money, boasters, proud, blasphemers, disobedient to parents, unthankful, unholy, unloving, unforgiving, slanderers, without self-control, brutal, despisers of good, traitors, headstrong, haughty, lovers of pleasure rather than lovers of God, having a form of godliness but denying its power. And from such people turn away" (**2 Tim. 3:1-5**).

Isn't it interesting that the Apostle Paul said, *"Know this...!"* It shouldn't come as a surprise to us that people today are self-centered, ungrateful, angry, and unforgiving. Many love pleasure and mock true righteousness. Some are religious, but deny the power of God; they have not embraced the cross and resurrection of Jesus Christ. Too often this is true even of believers. They love Jesus but have not submitted to His lordship.

Self-centered generation

The Millennial Generation (people born between 1980–1994) has been described as "Generation Me"—or, as the title of a 2013 *TIME* magazine article says, "The Me, Me, Me Generation." Today's younger people have grown up in an electronics-filled world that is increasingly socially networked. They have a strong focus on self, which finds its ultimate expression in the "selfie" (a photo taken of oneself with a smartphone and usually posted on social media). Narcissism (the preoccupation with self) has progressed to Narcissistic Hedonism where personal pleasure and fulfillment is the chief concern of those buying into it.

Many Western Millennials are affected by indulgence, self-centeredness, and radical, leftist ideology, which often revolves around feelings. Some can withstand the pressure to become like the world around them, but many fall prey to it.

Is this generation healthier emotionally and happier with its self-focus? A 2016 survey found that since 1990, rates of depression and anxiety among young people have increased by 70 percent. Suicide is the third leading cause of death among college students today.

A 2012 article on the *Healthline* website said: "Depression is an epidemic among college students. One out of every four suffers from some form of mental illness, including depression. Among college students, 44 percent report having symptoms of depression, and 75 percent do not seek help for mental health problems." We think we are more connected today with our plethora of social media, but loneliness is at an all-time high.

As believers in Jesus, we should be different from the world, yet many of us are also self-focused. We talk about ourselves *far* too much. We speak of our self-image and self-fulfillment, which point to self-love. We put the details of our daily lives on Facebook, talk about our accomplishments, and share the worries we have about the future. We compare ourselves with others and complain about those who have disappointed us. Even criticizing ourselves indicates a preoccupation with self. Our busy social networks give an indication as to our self-absorption.

Author and theologian A.W. Tozer said, "Self is the opaque veil that hides the face of God from us." Self-centeredness prevents us from discerning God's voice easily and obeying Him quickly. The sins of self-pity, self-righteousness, and pride dwell deeply within most of us. We are often unaware of them until the Holy Spirit brings them to our attention. These sins lead to greater sins, like self-promotion, jealousy, envy, and bitterness.

Esteem others

Philippians 2:3-7 says, *"Let nothing be done through selfish ambition or conceit, but in lowliness of mind let each esteem others better than himself. Let each of you look out not only for his own interests, but also for the interests of others. Let this mind be in you which was also in Christ Jesus, who, being in the form of God, did not consider it robbery to be equal with God, but made Himself of no reputation, taking the form of a bondservant, and coming in the likeness of men."*

Love of self comes naturally to us all, but once we are born again, the love of Christ should constrain us (2 Cor. 5:14). Then, we no longer serve ourselves first; we prefer and esteem others above ourselves.

"For the death that He died, He died to sin once for all; but the life that He lives He lives to God. Likewise you also, reckon yourselves to be dead indeed to sin, but alive to God in Christ Jesus our Lord." (**Rom. 6:10-11**).

94

The key to dying to self is in verse 11. We are to consider (reckon) ourselves as dead to reputation and sin. We reckon ourselves as dead to selfishness, self-love, and self-pity. We die to our carnal nature. What we would like to retain for ourselves may very well be the thing that God asks us to give up. To be empty of self, our lives need to be filled with and wrapped up in the life of God! *Jesus* is our center; through Him, we live and move and have our being (Acts 17:28).

Practical ways to love

"By this we know love, because He laid down His life for us. And we also ought to lay down our lives for the brethren. But whoever has this world's goods, and sees his brother in need, and shuts up his heart from him, how does the love of God abide in him? My little children, let us not love in word or in tongue, but in deed and in truth" (**1 John 3:16-18**).

There are countless ways we can lay down our lives in love for others. Here are just a few:

- Intercede for people! Prayer is hard work, but we need to give ourselves to it.
- Serve in every way possible. Prefer others. Refuse to control people and situations.
- Be accessible, even if it means giving up your time and privacy.
- Honor those in authority: government leaders, pastors, parents, and husbands.
- Forgive! Extend mercy, absorb the humiliation and hurt, and refuse to get revenge.
- Choose not to spend money frivolously on yourself so that you can give to the poor and to missions. Buy second-hand items so you can give generously.

Thomas à Kempis wrote, "No man is richer, no man more powerful, no man more free, than he who is able to leave himself and all things, and to set himself in the lowest place.

Let's replace the negatives of 2 Timothy 3:2-5 with corresponding positives that should be strong and growing in us. Let's fervently love the Lord and others. Let's not be greedy; let's live simply with eternity in mind. Let's be humble and not brag or blaspheme.

Let's be submissive, obedient, thankful, and holy. Let's love and forgive, and speak well of others. Let's control ourselves, be gentle and caring, and love what is good. Let's be loyal and faithful, and love God over pleasure. Let's not be entangled with this world but walk in godliness and in the power of the Holy Spirit!

Enemies of the cross

"For many walk... now tell you even weeping, that they are the enemies of the cross of Christ: whose end is destruction, whose god is their belly, and whose glory is in their shame—who set their mind on earthly things. For our citizenship is in heaven..." (**Phil. 3:18-20a**).

Paul says I'm *weeping* as I tell you of people who are enemies of the cross of Christ. They will *not* carry their cross and die to self. Instead, they serve their belly (food), they glory in their shame (what should shame them they take pride in), and they set their minds on earthly things. But *our* citizenship is in Heaven! We should not live like the world, share its values, or resist the crucified life. We are to be living sacrifices unto God.

Let the cross be our glory

Steve Fry composed a song entitled "Let It Be Said of Us" for the Promise Keepers ministry in 1994. As you read the words of this song, pray that they will be true for you.

> Let it be said of us that the Lord was our passion,
> That with gladness we bore every cross we were given.
> That we fought the good fight, that we finished the course;
> Knowing within us the power of the risen Lord.
>
> Let it be said of us we were marked by forgiveness;
> We were known by our love and delighted in meekness.
> We were ruled by His peace, heeding unity's call;
> Joined as one body that Christ would be seen by all.
>
> Let the cross be our glory and the Lord be our song.
> By mercy made holy, by the Spirit made strong.
> Let the cross be our glory and the Lord be our song
> Till the likeness of Jesus be through us made strong.
> Let the cross be our glory and the Lord be our song!

Chapter 17

MINISTRY OF ENCOURAGEMENT

"Let us hold fast the confession of our hope without wavering, for He who promised is faithful. And let us consider one another in order to stir up love and good works, not forsaking the assembling of ourselves together, as is the manner of some, but exhorting one another, and so much the more as you see the Day approaching" (**Heb. 10:23-25**).

A modern parable

One day the devil was exhibiting and selling some of his tools. They were priced according to their value. A buyer, looking at the tools, saw one labeled, 'greed' for $20, one labeled 'lust' for $50, and another called 'fear' for $100. Then he saw a very worn tool. Curious, he picked it up and finding no label or price, asked, "How much is this?" Satan answered, "Oh, that's one of my prized tools. I use it against believers and unbelievers alike. It's very effective. Sorry, it's not for sale." The man asked, "What is it?" The devil answered, "That tool is discouragement."

Discouragement comes knocking (or banging!) when you've given your best, and your best wasn't good enough. You are left with little strength and energy to keep going. Your hope and faith have diminished, and you feel worn out, oppressed, even depressed.

Victims of discouragement usually battle with condemnation and false guilt. The enemy whispers lies to them, causing them to question the truth about themselves, others, and God. He accuses their works and character. These accusations penetrate deeply into their souls, prompting negative reactions in their physical health.

The ministry of encouragement

Part of our wisdom in the Body of Christ is to assess the enemy's plans in order to beat him at his own game. We need to recognize the devil's strategy of discouraging believers, and war against those attacks through encouraging and affirming them. Instead of fearing the negative, we need to strengthen the positive.

The ministry of encouragement is one to which we are all called. In the Bible, we are commanded to exhort, strengthen, comfort, and encourage one another.

2 Corinthians 1:3-4 says, *"Blessed be the God and Father of our Lord Jesus Christ, the Father of mercies and God of all comfort, who comforts us in all our tribulation, that we may be able to comfort those who are in any trouble, with the comfort with which we ourselves are comforted by God."*

The Greek word translated as *comfort* is **paraklesis**. It implies help that is like "strength intensive as steel to the backbone." To comfort another is to come alongside him to put steel into his backbone and help him walk upright. Many of the promises in God's Word mention the Lord going through our trials and tribulations with us. He doesn't always protect us from difficulty, but He is always with us in the midst of it.

Consider the analogy of a back brace: the brace does not remove the physical damage in a person's back, but it does help ease the pain. We can do this for one another in the Body of Christ. We cannot remove all pain or change all difficult circumstances, but we can come alongside others in their trials. We can brace and support them in the difficulties they face.

Speaking words of courage to others is a powerful spiritual weapon. We wage warfare against the enemy by building up what he is trying to tear down. The devil seeks to divide and weaken God's people through slander and accusation. We need to take the opposing position of believing and speaking the best of others; we need to affirm, and pray for them. We need to instill confidence in them so that they can fulfill their purpose in the Lord.

Strengthen relationships

"From [Jesus], the whole body, joined and knit together by what every joint supplies, according to the effective working by which every part does its share, causes growth of the body for the edifying of itself in love" (**Eph. 4:16**). Joints are where two bones come together. The strength of the limb is in the joint more than in the individual bones. The way the limb functions depends on the joint. We need to build strong joints (relationships) in the family of God. No matter how strong we are separately, it is in our unity and co-working that we are most effective.

It is to our wisdom to build genuine relationships of harmony, trust, and interdependence. Our unity will invoke God's blessing (Ps. 133:1) and prove to the world that Jesus is the Messiah (John 17:21).

In these Last Days, we must continually be filled with God's Spirit. We read instructions on that in Ephesians 5. We do that by encouraging each other with life-giving words, and having hearts of thanks and praise. In the fear of God, we are to submit to one another, building and strengthening the Body of Christ (Eph. 5:18-21).

Simple ways to encourage

Encouraging others is not difficult. Anyone can affirm the people around them. We don't even need to know those we encourage; we can speak words of life to strangers as well as to family members or friends. Here are a few ways to bless others verbally:

1. Express Appreciation – Everyone wants to be appreciated. Notice and appreciate good works or service. If we fail to be grateful, we move from the position of the servant to the served; we expect to be waited on. That should never happen to us as believers. We need to be grateful for everything we receive, and we must express that gratitude. *"Thank you for that delicious meal." "I appreciate the time you spend preparing to teach." "Thank you for leading worship."*

2. Show loyalty – Besides speaking words of grace to those we are with, we should speak words of grace *about* others when they are absent. **James 4:11** says, *"Do not speak evil of one another, brethren."* Are the names of your family members, neighbors, friends, and leaders (civil, national, and spiritual) safe in your mouth? Benjamin Franklin said, "I will speak ill of no one, but will speak all the good I know of everyone."

3. Give affirmation – Praise nourishes the soul. Some people believe words of affirmation cause pride. But affirmation doesn't go to the head; it goes to the heart. We need to commend the goodness and godliness that we see in others. We can say: *"I enjoy being with you. Your love for Jesus makes me want to be more like Him." "The way you express God's kindness is beautiful!"*

99

Encourage yourself in the Lord

What about when *we* need encouragement? Do we wait for others to reach out to us? No, we go to the Lord for comfort. **Psalm 46:1** says, *"God is our refuge and strength, a very present help in trouble."* The phrase *a very present help in trouble* means God has proven Himself to be a reliable stronghold in the past, so we have no reason to fear.

As we proceed into the Last Days and experience more difficulties and hardships, we must know how to encourage ourselves in the Lord. We cannot afford to depend on someone else to do that. We need to fill ourselves with God's presence and joy by abiding in Him so that we have a surplus of His life to share with those in need.

In 1 Samuel 30, we read the story of when David desperately needed comfort and encouragement. The men around him were angry to the point of stoning him. No one encouraged him! So he strengthened himself in the Lord.

"...The Amalekites had invaded the South and Ziklag, attacked Ziklag and burned it with fire, and had taken captive the women and those who were there, from small to great; they did not kill anyone, but carried them away... David and his men came to the city, and there it was, burned with fire; and their wives, their sons and daughters had been taken captive. Then David, and the people who were with him, lifted up their voices and wept until they had no more power to weep. And David's two wives, Ahinoam and Abigail had been taken captive. David was greatly distressed, for the people spoke of stoning him, because the soul of all the people was grieved, every man for his sons and his daughters. But David strengthened himself in the Lord his God" (**1 Sam. 30:1b-6**).

David had lost his family, and then his comrades turned against him. They even spoke of killing him. What did David do? *He strengthened himself in the Lord.* He remembered God's faithfulness. He reflected on His track record of miraculously saving him in the past. He thought of God's kindness and mercy. He remembered His compassion and unfailing love. By reflecting on who God is and how He had cared for him before, David drew strength and courage. Next, he called the priest with the ephod and inquired of the Lord.

100

When he received God's answer to pursue and recover all, he went with his 600 men to attack the Amalekites. David's courage and reliance upon God inspired courage in the other men. They pursued the enemy with David and recovered all as God had promised – they came home with their wives and children and the spoil.

The situation had appeared dire until David encouraged himself in the Lord. Don't wait for others to encourage you. Stir yourself up to get a hold of God! Remember His track record of faithfulness, kindness, powerful rescue, and wisdom. Praise Him in faith that He will meet your needs, and that His grace is sufficient for you until your circumstances change. Strengthen yourself in the Lord!

Give while grieving

When Jesus heard that John the Baptist had been martyred, He went away to grieve. But when He saw the multitude of needy people, He began to teach them. Even in His grief, He was concerned for others.

In the same way, God often gives us opportunities to serve others when we are suffering. We can selfishly refuse to because we don't feel like it, or we can put aside our pain, and reach out in compassion. Part of our commitment to the Lord is to be available for Him to use us when and as He desires—even when we are hurting ourselves.

Most often, it is those who have gone through severe trials and received comfort from God who can best attend to the wounded and grieving. Suffering qualifies us to minister deeply and effectively. Rather than be a hindrance to anointed ministry, our past pain can be an asset. We need to allow God to use our sufferings for His purposes.

Comfort and exhort

Those who run marathons know that as they near the end of a long race, their legs ache, their throats burn, and their bodies scream for them to stop. This is when friends and fans are most valuable. Their encouragement helps them push through the pain to the finish line. In the same way, we are to help one another, so that we all can finish our race with joy!

We need to get alongside the hurting and infuse strength into their backbones! We probably can't remove their pain, but we can comfort them and lighten their load. We can urge them to remain steadfast as they trust in God.

We need to exhort one another to walk tall in Jesus, to run the race well, and to finish the course that the Lord has laid out for us. Let's speak words of life, courage, hope, and faith to those who desperately need to hear them. Let's intentionally build the Body of Christ.

God's words to Joshua have strengthened countless people over many centuries. They still offer encouragement and comfort today: *"Be strong and of good courage; do not be afraid, nor be dismayed, for the Lord your God is with you wherever you go"* (**Josh. 1:9**).

Chapter 18

THE IMMINENT RETURN OF THE LORD

"Immediately after the tribulation of those days the sun will be darkened, and the moon will not give its light; the stars will fall from heaven, and the powers of the heavens will be shaken. Then the sign of the Son of Man will appear in heaven, and then all the tribes of the earth will mourn. They will see the Son of Man coming on the clouds of heaven with power and great glory. And He will send His angels with a great sound of a trumpet, and they will gather together His elect from the four winds, from one end of heaven to the other... This generation will by no means pass away till all these things take place. Heaven and earth will pass away, but My words will by no means pass away" (**Matt. 24:29-31, 34-35**).

As we near the Day of the Lord, we are seeing a sharp increase of the signs Jesus predicted in Matthew 24. When all these signs accelerate at the *same time* and reach their peak together, we can know that we are living in the season of Jesus' return. The signs of Jesus' coming will continue to escalate until they simultaneously culminate in almost a volcanic eruption.

In 2017, Mike Bickle, founder of the International House of Prayer in Kansas City, speaking about the generation alive to see Jesus' return, said:

> "Scripture highlights this generation *much more* than all the others. God's plan related to the generation in which the Lord returns is the main focus in over 150 chapters in the Bible. Some of the prophecies in these chapters have been partially fulfilled, but await a complete fulfillment related to Jesus' return. The generation of His return will have unique dynamics—unprecedented pressures (shaking, sin, darkness) and an unprecedented outpouring of the Spirit and revival."

"For thus says the Lord of hosts: '...I will shake heaven and earth, the sea and dry land; and I will shake all nations, and they shall come to the Desire of All Nations [Jesus]...' " (**Hag. 2:6-7**).

Everything Jesus said about the days leading up to His return *will* be fulfilled. We need to know and understand His warnings and predictions so that we can live carefully and wisely. We must wear spiritual armor, watch and pray, and love one another fervently while doing the work of an evangelist and fulfilling our ministries (1 Pet. 4:7-8, 2 Tim. 4:5)!

Jesus is coming back for a holy Bride that adores Him and is sharing His love with others. He wants to wash her of worldly dust, lust, and unrighteous behavior. He is setting her apart for Himself. *"...Christ loved the church and gave Himself for her, that He might sanctify and cleanse her with the washing of water by the word, that He might present her to Himself a glorious church, not having spot or wrinkle or any such thing, but that she should be holy, without blemish"* (**Eph. 5:25b-27**).

The Lord's Bride will be spotlessly pure. She'll be without a wrinkle, perpetually youthful. Many of the present older generation will experience renewal as they wait upon the Lord in these days (Isa. 40:31). They will be able to lead the younger generation through the hardships ahead, and the Holy Spirit will anoint them to help bring revival to the Church.

Learn the Scriptures

As we meditate on the Scriptures, the Holy Spirit will deepen our intimacy with God and tell us what He is saying *now*. We must be obedient to the Word so that we don't fall into deception. We must let it renew our minds and transform our lives. We are to live *"by every word that proceeds from the mouth of God"* (**Matt. 4:4**). Our lives should revolve around God's written Word and His spoken words to our hearts. We need to give ourselves to studying the Word of God; it will instruct, correct, and equip us for every good work. *"All Scripture is given by inspiration of God, and is profitable for doctrine, for reproof, for correction, for instruction in righteousness, that the man of God may be complete, thoroughly equipped for every good work"* (**2 Tim. 3:16-17**).

Needed: people who understand and instruct

"And those of the people who understand shall instruct many" (**Dan. 11:33**). In the Lord's mercy, He will raise up Bible teachers and mentors who will help others understand the Scriptures related to the end times.

Many will be hungry for answers from God's Word. It is vital that we know what the Word says and be able and willing to explain it to others. We need to understand that we are called to prepare and equip generations.

" *'Behold, the days are coming,' says the Lord God, 'That I will send a famine on the land, not a famine of bread, nor a thirst for water, but of hearing the words of the Lord' "* (**Amos 8:11**). There *will be* a famine regarding the Word of the Lord in the Last Days, but let's not let it happen in our homes, neighborhoods, or spheres of authority. We need to know and declare God's Word!

We must prepare for the future with vision and strategy. Although Jesus may come for us sooner rather than later, we will still go through difficult times. Most of the Body of Christ around the world are *already* enduring tribulation! The future may appear overwhelming if we view it with natural eyes only, but if we will tackle one day at a time with God's grace and strength, we need not be anxious. Even in turbulent and demanding times, we can rest in Him and let His presence guide and sustain us.

Corrie Ten Boom was known for saying, "When a train goes through a tunnel and it gets dark, you don't throw away the ticket and jump off. You sit still and trust the engineer."

Anticipate His return

As we near Jesus' return, we must be watching for Him and actively serving Him. How terrible it will be for those who are not looking for Him and are not prepared when He comes! Although in some ways, life appears to be continuing as usual right now, in reality, things are changing fairly quickly. Jesus gave us a clear warning in **Matthew 24:42,44**: *"Watch… for you do not know what hour your Lord is coming… be ready, for the Son of Man is coming at an hour you do not expect."*

Because we don't know when Jesus will come, we must be ready at all times. The apostle Paul wrote: *"For the Lord Himself will descend from heaven with a shout, with the voice of an archangel, and with the trumpet of God. And the dead in Christ will rise first. Then we who are alive and remain shall be caught up together with them in the clouds to meet the Lord in the air. And thus we shall always be with the Lord…*

For you yourselves know perfectly that the day of the Lord so comes as a thief in the night. For when they say, 'Peace and safety!' then sudden destruction comes upon them, as labor pains upon a pregnant woman. And they shall not escape. But you, brethren, are not in darkness, so that this Day should overtake you as a thief. You are all sons of light and sons of the day. We are not of the night, nor of darkness. Therefore let us not sleep, as others do, but let us watch and be sober" (**1 Thess. 4:16-5:6**).

Hasten the day of the Lord

The apostles Peter and Paul had the same revelation concerning the Day of the Lord. Peter wrote, *"The day of the Lord will come as a thief in the night, in which the heavens will pass away with a great noise, and the elements will melt with fervent heat; both the earth and the works that are in it will be burned up. Therefore, since all these things will be dissolved, what manner of persons ought you to be in holy conduct and godliness, looking for and hastening the coming of the day of God... Looking forward to these things, be diligent to be found by Him in peace, without spot and blameless... Since you know this beforehand, beware lest you also fall from your own steadfastness, being led away with the error of the wicked; but grow in the grace and knowledge of our Lord and Savior Jesus Christ..."* (**2 Pet. 3:10-12a, 14-15a, 17-18a**).

Can we actually hasten the day of the Lord? Yes, there are some things we can do. Here are a few: (1) If we are holy before the Lord, diligent to be at peace and blameless, we can hasten His coming. (2) If we preach the gospel in all nations, we move His coming forward. Matthew 24:14 says the end will come after the gospel is preached in all nations. (3) If we repent and encourage others to repent, His coming will be sooner. Acts 3:19-21 says repentance and conversion are part of all things being restored.

There may be other ways we can hasten the Jesus' return, but for sure we know to do these three things: preach the gospel of the kingdom everywhere, engage in repentance toward God as a lifestyle, and walk in holiness and be blameless before the Lord.

In anticipation of Jesus' return, we need to diligently grow in grace and in knowing the Lord intimately, so that we are able to stand steadfastly in truth and to discern and refuse error.

By God's grace and with the help of the Holy Spirit, may we have the same testimony that Paul had: *"I have fought the good fight, I have finished the race, I have kept the faith. Finally, there is laid up for me the crown of righteousness, which the Lord, the righteous Judge, will give to me on that Day, and not to me only but also to all who have loved His appearing"* (**2 Tim. 4:7-8**).

Let's finish *our* race and keep the faith! Let's love His appearing and hasten His return!

"Now to Him who is able to keep you from stumbling, and to present you faultless before the presence of His glory with exceeding joy, to God our Savior, Who alone is wise, be glory and majesty, dominion and power, both now and forever. Amen" (**Jude 1: 23-24**)

Made in the USA
Monee, IL
23 September 2021